# PETERSON'S

## The Insider's Guide to

# PAYING FOR COLLEGE

## Find Out How to Get More Money for College!

*Endorsed by College Parents of America*

### DON BETTERTON
Director of Undergraduate Financial Aid
at Princeton University

**P** **Peterson's**
Thomson Learning™

Australia • Canada • Denmark • Japan • Mexico • New Zealand • Philippines
Puerto Rico • Singapore • Spain • United Kingdom • United States

**About Peterson's**

Founded in 1966, Peterson's, a division of Thomson Learning, is the nation's largest and most respected provider of lifelong learning online resources, software, reference guides, and books. The Education Supersite$^{SM}$ at petersons.com—the Web's most heavily traveled education resource—has searchable databases and interactive tools for contacting U.S.-accredited institutions and programs. CollegeQuest$^{SM}$ (CollegeQuest.com) offers a complete solution for every step of the college decision-making process. GradAdvantage$^{TM}$ (GradAdvantage.org), developed with Educational Testing Service, is the only electronic admissions service capable of sending official graduate test score reports with a candidate's online application. Peterson's serves over 55 million education consumers annually.

Thomson Learning is among the world's largest providers of lifelong learning information. Headquartered in Stamford, CT, with multiple offices worldwide, Thomson Learning is a division of The Thomson Corporation (TTC), one of the world's leading information companies. TTC operates mainly in the U.S., Canada, and the UK and has annual revenues of over US$6 billion. The Corporation's common shares are traded on the Toronto, Montreal, and London stock exchanges. For more information, visit TTC's Internet address at www.thomcorp.com.

Visit Peterson's Education Center on the Internet (World Wide Web) at www.petersons.com

**Library of Congress Cataloging-in-Publication Data**

Betterton, Don M., 1938–
    Insider's guide to paying for college / by Don M. Betterton.
       p. cm.
    ISBN 0-7689-0230-4
    1. Student aid—United States. 2. College costs—United States.  I. Title.
LB2337.4.B49  1999
378.3'0973—dc21
                                                        99-056877
                                                        CIP

Printed in Canada

10  9  8  7  6  5  4  3  2  1

# CONTENTS

# INTRODUCTION

- About this book
- No false claims, no tricks
- The Internet connection
- Keeping up with current information
- If you aren't on line
- Who should read the *Insider's Guide?*
- How to use the *Insider's Guide*
- This is a financial aid book
- If you still have questions

## ABOUT THIS BOOK

This book is titled *Insider's Guide To Paying For College* for good reason. I have thirty years' experience in the financial aid field and deal with the subject matter on a daily basis. I don't want to criticize other books on financial aid—in fact many of them are quite good. But typically they are written by an author with a background in financial planning who has taken the time to learn about student aid procedures as a subcategory of how families manage their money.

While such books are often thorough and accurate, they lack the perspective of someone who has extensive hands-on experience in dealing with actual parents and students who are trying to navigate the aid process.

This is not a financial aid encyclopedia. Both you and I would be bored if I tried to explain financial aid in detail. My intention is to be clear and concise—to summarize the relevant topic, to give advice, and to refer you to Internet sites for more information.

I hope that my experience in the field will add value to the book's contents. The goal is to have you truly understand how financial aid works. It will then be your job to fit your own family situation into this framework. If we are both successful, by the time the process is over, you should feel as though you are getting your fair share of available financial aid.

## NO FALSE CLAIMS, NO TRICKS

Some aid publications say they will find you a scholarship that otherwise would go begging. Others promise to get you more money by teaching you the tricks to filling out an aid application. If only financial aid were that simple.

The few scholarships that go begging do so because they are so highly restricted that hardly anyone meets the requirements.

> ***Insider's Tip:*** When it comes to completing the Free Application for Federal Student Aid (FAFSA), there really are no tricks, at least not any that will not make you nervous when you sign the FAFSA and certify that you didn't give false or misleading information.

There are, however, some things I can tell you about how the data you submit are used in the federal need formula. With that knowledge, you can look at your family's financial situation and decide how to present your information in a way that maximizes your eligibility for aid. In Chapter 5, Reducing the Toll II: How to Find Grants and Other Need Aid, I give you advice on useful (and legal) strategies that will do this.

## THE INTERNET CONNECTION

You are encouraged to take advantage of the Internet references. Many of these sites are the primary source of program information. Should you want more detail, you can find it on the Internet. Furthermore, since financial aid rules change frequently, these sites are usually the best sources for the latest program descriptions.

There are a handful of Internet sites that contain the majority of good information about financial aid. These are listed as a group in Chapter 3, Before You Enter the Highway: Getting Off to a Good Start. This is a helpful reference if you would like to browse through the Web pages and see what topics interest you.

At other points in the *Insider's Guide,* when the subject matter deals with a specific issue that is covered more thoroughly on the Internet, there is a reference to the appropriate site and a step-by-step guide that takes you to the exact location.

## KEEPING UP WITH CURRENT INFORMATION

This book is designed to be used in conjunction with the Internet, which will keep you up-to-date on the constantly changing college financial aid scene.

The information contained on these pages is current as of September 1999, and much of it is aimed at students who will be college freshmen beginning in fall 2000.

For those of you who are looking farther down the road, the Web site will be updated yearly, beginning in the winter of 1999–2000. All you need to do is to go to http://insiders. petersons.com where the most current information will be shown. These free updates are a valuable bonus for you and the reason why we say that the *Insider's Guide* is the only financial aid book you'll ever need.

## IF YOU AREN'T ON LINE

If you don't have Internet access, this book will still provide you with helpful financial aid information. You will, however, lack some of the detail that can be found on the Internet. You also will miss out on the *Insider's Guide* Web site, which will give readers yearly updates on the changes that occur in financial aid.

My suggestion is that you make a note of the Internet addresses that contain information that is most important to you. You can then use the computer in your school or town library to see what these sites have to offer. Later on in the year, you can do the same thing to access the *Insider's Guide* Web site, where new information will be provided.

## WHO SHOULD READ THE *INSIDER'S GUIDE?*

The primary audience for this book is the typical college-going family—parents with a dependent child who plans to enroll as an undergraduate. As used in this book, the word *"you"* can mean either the parents or the student.

However, since a large percentage of today's college students are not 18- to 22-year-old dependents, Chapter 8, Side Roads: Nontraditional Students, explains different rules for part-time students, independent (including military veterans) students, graduate students, and distance learners.

Scholarship opportunities for members of minority groups, women, and disabled students can be found in Chapter 4, Reducing the Toll I: How to Find Scholarships.

Special financial aid rules for children with divorced or separated parents are contained in Chapter 5, Reducing the Toll II: How to Find Grants and Other Need Aid.

## HOW TO USE THE *INSIDER'S GUIDE*

After you finish with this introduction, you should read Chapter 1, An Aerial-View Road Map of Your Route, to get a feel for the book's contents.

From that point on, it's up to you. My suggestion is that you read through the rest of the book so you understand fully the many different aspects of what it takes to pay for a college education, from organizing an early savings plan to making that final payment on a student loan. The summary of key points at the end of each chapter should help with this overview.

If you have three or more years until your child enrolls in college, Chapter 2, Preparing For Your Trip: Start a Savings Plan, is the place to begin.

I expect, however, that most of you will purchase the *Insider's Guide* during your child's junior or senior year in high school. In this case, Chapter 3, Before You Enter the Highway: Getting Off to a Good Start, and the chapters that follow contain the core information that you will need.

## THIS IS A FINANCIAL AID BOOK

This publication deals with the subject of how to pay for college. Obviously, whatever plans you make in regard to paying for college go hand-in-hand with proper academic preparation and a well-thought-out admission plan.

If the process of choosing the proper curriculum, preparing for the SAT or ACT, and organizing your college list is not already underway, there are a number of Internet sites that give good advice and offer to help you fill out your applications.

Among these, one of the best is CollegeQuest, which was developed by Peterson's, a Thomson Learning Company, at http://www.collegequest.com. The College Board's home page at http://www.collegeboard.org has links to both admission and aid information, and they are in the process of adding new features.

## IF YOU STILL HAVE QUESTIONS

There's lots of good information contained in the following pages, and every family should benefit by becoming more knowledgeable about how the financial aid system works. But in the end, applying for and receiving aid is an individual matter.

After you've read the *Insider's Guide,* you may have questions about where to get started, what is the status of your application, or how to explain your special circumstances. Fortunately, there are a number of different places you can go to get answers to questions like these. Among them are your high school guidance counselor, the help lines at the application processing centers, and college financial aid administrators. There is even the option of asking questions of aid experts through the Internet. All of these possibilities are explained in Chapter 9, If You Still Have Questions.

# CHAPTER 1

# An Aerial-View Road Map of Your Route

- If you have a young child
- Financial aid fundamentals
- A scholarship is the best aid of all
- There are more need-based grants than merit scholarships
- After your child has been admitted
- Once the college decision has been made
- If you are a nontraditional student
- If you want to know more

A teaching principle is to tell your students where you are going before you start and to give them some idea what they will learn when they get there. With this in mind, here is a map of where this book will take you.

## IF YOU HAVE A YOUNG CHILD . . .

then it's off to Chapter 2, Preparing for Your Trip: Start A Savings Plan. Before it's time to turn your attention to the financial aid process, you can learn why you should save and how to go about it. Here you will find:

1. The reasons for saving
2. Why you should start early
3. In whose name to save
4. The importance of a regular savings routine

5. How much to put aside

6. Internet sites for college cost and savings calculators

7. Savings plan options

8. A checklist for savers

**Some things you will learn**

- It is to your advantage to put money aside for college and to start saving as early as you can. The length of time that your money builds is as important as how much you contribute each month.

- Rather than being penalized for saving, you will be rewarded. If you qualify for aid, the need formula will ask for less from your savings account than the yearly interest you earn—if you pay attention to the advice that I give in this chapter.

- It may not be wise to put your money in a prepaid or guaranteed tuition plan.

# FINANCIAL AID FUNDAMENTALS

Some of the comments I hear about financial aid show a good understanding of the subject. But more often than not, misconceptions abound. There are also some basic financial aid facts you should know. For both reasons, it is important for you to read Chapter 3, Before You Enter the Aid Highway: Getting Off to a Good Start. Here you will find:

1. Clearing up misconceptions

2. The purpose of financial aid

3. Financial aid by the numbers

4. Why these numbers are important to you

5. The truth about college costs

6. The top financial aid Internet sites

**Some things you will learn**

- Don't believe everything your neighbor tells you about financial aid.

- Scholarships based on merit account for only about 8 percent of all financial aid.
- College costs may be high, but they're probably lower than you think.

## A SCHOLARSHIP IS THE BEST AID OF ALL

It is free money, and you don't have to demonstrate financial need to receive a scholarship. To learn more, go to Chapter 4, Reducing the Toll I: How to Find Scholarships. Here you will find:

1. The different kinds of gift aid
2. Education benefits
3. Where to look for scholarships
4. Take a personal inventory
5. The importance of starting early
6. Scholarships for people who are disabled, members of minority groups, and women

**Some things you will learn**

- Don't wait until your child is in the twelfth grade to think about how he or she is going to win a scholarship. Wouldn't it be good to know if your state (like Florida) gives a $2,000 scholarship if your child has a 3.5 GPA, $1,500 for a 3.2 GPA, and $0 below a 3.2? Imagine how much attention you would pay to that report card.
- Free scholarship searches look for the same awards as searches that charge a fee.
- The strength of your academic record may effect how much need-based grant you receive from a college.

## THERE ARE MORE NEED-BASED GRANTS THAN MERIT SCHOLARSHIPS

Completing the aid application (or applications) can be complicated; information on this process is found in Chapter 5, Reducing the Toll II: How to Find Grants and Other Need Aid. Here you will find:

1. How to determine if you might qualify for need aid
2. Estimate your Expected Family Contribution (EFC)
3. Estimate college costs
4. Estimate your need
5. Learn about college aid policies
6. The aid applications
7. Awarding financial aid

**Some things you will learn**

- If you plan to read this chapter, you probably should complete the Free Application for Federal Student Aid (FAFSA). Why? Because you want to know more about need aid, and 85 percent of all assistance starts with the FAFSA. Furthermore, it's free and should only take about an hour of your time to fill out.

- Odds are you won't win a merit scholarship, but you will take out a loan. This is not a reflection on your ability but a way to illustrate that 8 percent of students win scholarships, while nearly 60 percent borrow money.

- What steps to take to increase your eligibility for financial aid (that are legal and ethical).

# AFTER YOUR CHILD HAS BEEN ADMITTED . . .

there is important information in Chapter 6, Choosing a Destination: The Role of Aid in Selecting a College. Here you will find:

1. How to figure your cost of attendance
2. Determine how much good aid you have
3. Calculating your family financial responsibility
4. If you have a gap
5. Dealing with the financial aid office
6. If you are not receiving need aid

### Some things you will learn

- What colleges sometimes don't tell you—how much you actually have to pay

- The word is out—you can negotiate your financial aid award. The only problem is that the "word" is mostly wrong.

- Because College A is giving you more money than College B, it doesn't mean you are getting a better award.

## ONCE THE COLLEGE DECISION HAS BEEN MADE . . .

you will want to read Chapter 7, Paying the Toll: You've Selected a College, It's Time to Pay the Bill. This is where you find out if financial aid has actually worked for you, including:

1. An aid award checklist
2. Your student loan
3. Alternate aid sources
4. Payment plans
5. Tuition tax credits

### Some things you will learn

- If you receive an aid award letter, you don't really have the money until you do a number of other things. Do you know what they are?

- If you borrow the $17,125 maximum Stafford undergraduate loan, one type will cost you $2,600 less than the other.

- If you need extra money to pay the bill, do you know where to look first?

## IF YOU ARE A NONTRADITIONAL STUDENT . . .

try Chapter 8, Side Roads: Nontraditional Students. There are as many part-time, adult, and graduate students as there are

18- to 22-year-old undergraduates, and some of the aid rules are different. Here you will find:

1. Aid for part-time students
2. Older undergraduates
3. Graduate students
4. Military veterans
5. Distance learning

**Some things you will learn**

- Don't expect to receive aid if you go to college less than one-half time.

- Even if you and your parents agree, you can't declare yourself independent for financial aid purposes.

- If you plan to be a graduate student, be prepared to borrow. Loans are more common for graduate students than they are for undergraduates.

## IF YOU WANT TO KNOW MORE . . .

Chapter 9, If You Still Have Questions, tells you how to get in touch with the people who can help you navigate through the financial aid process. Here you will find:

1. Where to go for free advice
2. Fee-based advice

**Some things you will learn**

- Almost all the aid advice you need is free.

- Who to call if you want to know why your FAFSA information has not been received by your college

- There are financial aid experts available to answer your e-mail questions.

# CHAPTER 2

# PREPARING FOR YOUR TRIP: START A SAVINGS PLAN

- Reasons for saving
- Start early
- In whose name to save
- Establish a regular savings routine
- How much to put aside
- What savings plan to choose
- Sponsors of guaranteed tuition and college savings plans
- A checklist for savers
- Summary of key points

Even though the college destination for your child may be far down the road, it's a good idea to develop a long-range financial plan. This means that you should start a savings program that considers both your financial condition and the likely college aspirations of your child.

## REASONS FOR SAVING

### You May Not Have to Apply for Aid

While the U.S. is justifiably proud of its $65 billion financial aid system that makes it possible for virtually any student to attend college, there are definite advantages if you can accumulate enough money to pay for college on your own. If you are well-off financially, your objective should be to save enough (in combination with what you can afford from income) so you can pay the college bill without applying for aid. Some of the advantages of not being "on aid" are:

- **The college application process is easier**. Keeping track of many different kinds of admission requirements and deadlines can be difficult by itself without adding the extra step of applying for aid.

- **Your child can avoid taking out loans.** Nearly every financial aid award includes a student loan that must be repaid for ten years after graduation. In some cases, the amount of loan to be repaid may effect career choice.

- **You won't have to deal with a gap.** If the college can't meet 100 percent of your financial need (when your award totals less than your need, the shortfall is the "gap"), you will have to come up with more than your expected family contribution. This can mean a parental loan in addition to the student loan. Parental loans have higher interest rates than student loans, and repayment of the principal begins right away.

- **Merit scholarships mean extra money.** If you are not receiving need aid and your child wins a merit scholarship, it will directly offset your contribution. For an aid recipient, an outside scholarship sometimes replaces other financial aid and does not reduce the parental contribution.

---

◇

## THE "TRY TO AVOID APPLYING FOR AID" PLAN

If you want to set up a plan with the intention of covering the full bill when it is time for your child to attend college, I recommend that you use a target figure based on out-of-state four-year public total cost.

For 1998–99, this number was $15,700, about half way between the cost of in-state public and private colleges. If it turns out that the college your child chooses is less expensive (or he or she wins a scholarship), you can use the money for another purpose. If the college costs more than you have accumulated, you will have to use a portion of your income, but this amount will be considerably less than you would have had to contribute if you didn't save.

Example: Assume you start saving when your child is 3 years old. You can use the calculators referred to in this chapter if you want to make other assumptions.

(a) Start with the $15,700 1998–99 cost.

(b) Inflate at 5 percent per year for fifteen years to get a freshman year cost of $32,600.

(c) Continue to increase the cost by 5 percent per year for the next three years of undergraduate study to get a total four-year cost of $140,700.

(d) To cover this amount, assuming a 6 percent return on your savings, you have to put aside $480 per month.

Of course $480 a month is not small change, and that amount is likely to be out of reach for most families. But it does illustrate an important point. When you read that a college education for your child will cost $140,700 in fifteen years, you think, "How can we ever afford that?" The answer is if you start to save early, you can afford it for about what many families spend on a payment for their second car.

———————————— ◇ ————————————

## Even if You Are an Aid Applicant, You are Better Off

If you are like most American families, the reality is that you cannot afford to save enough money to pay the full cost of college some years down the road. In this case, your goal should be to put aside as much as you reasonably can.

Although there is a popular misconception that families are penalized for saving, the truth is that you will be much better off if you accumulate money for college. The financial aid formula is kind to savers—that is, parental savers. See "In Whose Name to Save" later in this chapter.

> **How the need formula deals with parental assets:**
> Assume that by the time your child is ready to go to college, you have put aside $50,000. Although the exact amount varies with the parents' age, on average, the first $40,000 is protected. Of the $10,000 remaining, you will be asked to contribute about $500. At the same time, assuming you are earning 6 percent on your money, your $50,000 will grow to $53,000. After you have paid $500 to the college, you will end up with $52,500. The "penalty" is that you will have to use some of your interest accumulation to pay for college.

## It Is Better to Save Than Borrow

You will be far ahead in the long run by getting paid interest rather than paying interest. Since student and parent loans are the largest form of financial aid, it is likely that saving more will mean borrowing less. In terms of the bottom line, the difference is significant.

——————————— ◇ ———————————

### EXAMPLE

**The Jackson family** has not saved for college, and they have to borrow $10,000 per year for four years, a total of $40,000, from the federal PLUS loan program at 8 percent interest. With a ten-year repayment period, their obligation is $486 per month for 120 months, a total of $58,272. (*Note:* the Jacksons actually end up with only $38,400 because of the 4 percent origination fee, but we'll stay with the $40,000 for now.)

**The Smith family** planned ahead and began to save ten years before their 8-year-old daughter would start college. They put aside $245 each month ($2,940 per year) and received a 6 percent rate of return. Although they only contributed $29,400 during this time, the compounding of earned interest resulted in a nest egg of $40,000.

**The Jackson and the Smith families** followed different routes to contribute $40,000 to college.

**The Smiths** (the savers) paid $29,400 to get their $40,000.

**The Jacksons** (the borrowers) paid $58,272 to produce their $40,000.

Even if the Smiths qualify for aid, the asset protection allowance in the need formula would reduce their "countable" assets to zero, and they would not be asked to use any of their savings for college.

---- ◇ ----

## START EARLY

Given enough time, modest yearly contributions can add up to a quite large savings account. As a general rule, for every five years you wait to get started, you'll have to double your monthly savings amount to reach your goal.

---- ◇ ----

### EXAMPLE

**The Carter family** puts aside $1,000 per year ($76 per month) starting on their child's first birthday. Over seventeen years, they contribute a total of $17,000, which grows to $30,000 at a 6 percent interest rate when the child is ready for college.

**The Jones family** waits until their child is a freshman in high school and saves the same amount, $1,000 per year, for four years. When their child graduates from high school, their $4,000 is worth $4,600.

If the **Joneses** want to end up with the same amount of money as the **Carters**, they would have had to save $6,500 each year over the four-year period.

---- ◇ ----

> *Insider's advice:* If you plan to save, start as early as you can. If, like the Carters, you can afford the $76 per month (or more) on your child's first birthday, why wait?

# IN WHOSE NAME TO SAVE

## The System Favors Parental Saving

Because the need formula asks for a much larger share of student assets than parental assets, you have to decide who "owns" the money.

The formula specifies that, at most, 5.6 percent of parental savings are added to the contribution from income. (Because an asset protection allowance is subtracted before savings are looked at, the rate can be as low as 0 percent for assets below $40,000, gradually rising to the 5.6 percent contribution rate as assets increase.) For assets in the student's name, 35 percent of the total (with no protection allowance) is expected as a direct contribution.

─────────── ◇ ───────────

### EXAMPLE

**The Lee parents,** ten years before their child started college, bought a $30,000 zero-coupon bond that has a value of $50,000 when they report it as their only asset on the FAFSA. After the need formula is applied, they are asked to contribute $500 of this in the freshman year and about $500 each year after. Over four years, they will pay approximately $2,000.

**The Watson family** does the same thing but registers the bond in their child's name and reports the $50,000 as a student asset on the FAFSA. When the need formula is applied, the student is asked to contribute $17,500 for the freshman year and 35 percent of the declining balance for the next three years. Over four years, the student pays about $41,000.

This point bears repeating. In this example, over four years of undergraduate study, $2,000 is expected from the parents' $50,000, while $41,000 is expected from the student's $50,000. The $39,000 difference is offset to some extent by the fact that the parents will pay more in federal and state taxes than the student, but this amount is insignificant compared to what the need formula asks for.

———————————— ◇ ————————————

> ***Insider's advice:*** If you think you will be a candidate for aid, keep "family money" in the parents' name. You will lose more under the financial aid rules than you will gain from a reduction in federal and state taxes.
>
> This does not mean that your child's bank account balance should be zero. There is nothing wrong with keeping money from your child's earnings and gifts in his or her own name.
>
> This is the type of savings that the architects of the need formula had in mind when they set the 35 percent contribution rate on student assets. They did not anticipate that student aid applicants would hold large amounts of parental savings in their names.

### Another Reason for Saving in the Parents' Name

Besides the obvious financial advantage of not moving parental savings into the child's account, there is also the issue of who controls the money. In most states, at age 18, the child can determine how his or her money will be spent. If your child decides not to attend college, did you plan to pay for that new car? This is another factor to consider when you start a college savings plan.

## ESTABLISH A REGULAR SAVINGS ROUTINE

Don't make contributions to the college savings account an "on-again, off-again" arrangement. If being better prepared to pay for college is an important family goal, make regular deposits.

> *Insider's advice:* Make your college savings plan a priority and stick with contributions every month. Increase the amount as your earnings increase. Use a payroll deduction if possible.

## HOW MUCH TO PUT ASIDE

You can either set a future dollar amount as your goal or save what you can afford and check occasionally to see how much college tuition your savings will buy. Here are some of your options.

### Shoot For a Target Figure

If your approach is to aim for a future amount, don't make it too complicated. If you start saving early, you will know very little about the cost of the college your child will eventually attend. A good "middle of the road" strategy is to save enough to pay half the average tuition cost at a private college. Today, that figure is $7,500 per year (half of $15,000), or $30,000 over four years.

### EXAMPLE

The current four-year cost based on one-half private college tuition is $30,000. Assuming an eight-year-old with ten years to college and a 5 percent annual increase in college costs, $52,600 is your target figure. With a 6 percent rate of return, you need to save $320 per month.

### Save What You Can Afford

Another approach is to set aside what you can after you looking at your monthly income and expenses. For most families, this is the preferred method, since it is based on your own financial condition and not a guess about future college costs. Here are some ways to think about what you can afford to save:

- **The "budget" method**—take a portion of what you have left each month after you pay your bills.

- **The "percent of income" method**—10 percent of income is good place to start. Adjust this up or down based on your own situation.

- **The "replace spending with savings" method**—take the expense of an item you can do without and save the money instead.

However you decide to organize your savings plan—shooting for a target figure or saving what you can afford—there are easy-to-use calculators on the Internet that do the math for you.

―――――――――――――――◇―――――――――――――――

## COLLEGE COST AND SAVINGS PLAN CALCULATOR WEB SITES

- **http://www.finaid.org.** Click on "Calculators." There you will find "College Cost Projector," "Savings Plan Designer," and "Savings Growth Projector."

- **http://www.salliemae.com** Click on "Calculators." There you will find "Forecasting College Costs" and "Savings Calculators."

- **http://www. collegeboard.org** Click on "Students and Parents." Click on "Services." Click on "Financial Aid Calculators." There you will find "College Savings Calculator" (no college cost calculator).

―――――――――――――――◇―――――――――――――――

### Current College Costs

If you are going to tie your savings goal to the future college costs, you will have to start with current costs. To get these figures for individual colleges, go to http://www.collegequest. com. From the home page, click on "Pick," click on

"Alphabetical List of Colleges," and enter the colleges for which you would like to see current costs.

If you want to start with college costs by sector, here are the averages for 1998–99. (Total expenses include tuition, room and board, books, transportation, and other expenses.)

- Four-year public (in-state) — $10,458
- Four-year public (out-of-state) — $15,686
- Four-year private — $22,533
- Two-year private — $14,222
- Two-year public — $6,445

*Note:* These costs are for resident students, except for two-year public colleges where the costs are for a commuter (College Board, 1998).

## WHAT SAVINGS PLAN TO CHOOSE

This is an area in which I'm going to refrain from giving you advice. Where to invest your money (even if it is for future college expenses) does not fall under the field of financial aid. Except for pointing out some of the tax rules and how the need formula looks at family assets held in different accounts, I'll leave the investment decision up to you and your financial adviser.

Another reason not to give advice is that no single plan is right for every family.

———————— ◇ ————————

### EXAMPLE

**The Smith family** wants to guarantee tuition at the local public university (where the student plans to attend) at a future date and is willing to trade security for a possible higher rate of return. Their child plans to commute from home, so saving for room and board charges is not important.

**The Hanson family** wants to make sure their savings can be used for any college in the country, plans to put enough aside to cover room and board as well as tuition, and is willing to take some risks with their investment.

**The Smiths and the Hansons** have very different educational goals, and it is unlikely that they would choose the same savings plan.

Fortunately, there is enough variety in savings plans so both families can find the program that best meets their needs.

There are three types of savings plans:

1. Guaranteed or prepaid tuition
2. College savings
3. General savings that can be used for college

### Guaranteed or prepaid tuition

Through either a one-time payment or monthly installments, you buy all or part of tuition at its current rate. At a future date when the student enrolls, your purchase is good for the same percent of tuition at that time.

For example, assume the current tuition at your state university is $2,000 per year and your child is 8 years old. If you pay $8,000 now, you will receive a voucher that will cover four years of tuition in ten years when your child goes to college. When your child does enroll, you would cash in one voucher each year instead of paying tuition.

These plans are a "hedge" against inflation in tuition charges and are intended for students who will attend a public institution in their state. You do not have control over where your money is invested, but you are guaranteed a rate of return equal to the inflation in tuition costs.

If your child is uncertain about where he or she will go to college, check with the plan administrator to see what happens to your money if your child does not attend a state college or university. The tuition benefit that you prepaid may be reduced if the student goes to an in-state private college or an out-of-state institution.

## Tax status of guaranteed or prepaid tuition plans

As of September 1999, based on a recent IRS ruling, no federal and state taxes are due on the yearly income that your account earns. When you withdraw the money to pay college expenses, the amount is taxed at the student's rate. Some states exempt this income from any state tax. There is now a proposal before Congress to make the earnings on prepaid tuition plans tax free instead of tax deferred. Should changes like this occur, updated information will be posted on the *Insider's Guide* Internet site, available through http://www.petersons.com.

## Need formula treatment

The value of a guaranteed or prepaid tuition plan is not reported on the FAFSA, because the amount that you withdraw from the account in any given year is treated as a direct payment to the tuition bill.

For example, if you bought a full-tuition share when you entered the program ten years ago, today's tuition would be paid from your account, and the cost of attendance would be used in determining need would not include tuition. This means that under the need rules, there is a 100 percent "contribution rate" on a guaranteed tuition withdrawal. This is a much higher expectation than assets held in college or general savings plans.

---

*Insider's advice:* Be cautious about choosing the guaranteed or prepaid tuition savings option if you think you might apply for financial aid when it is time for your child to attend college.

---

## College Savings

These are programs without a direct tie-in to the cost of tuition. These plans permit you to set a savings goal for the total cost of any college that your child is interested in attending. With a college savings plan, there is usually no restriction on where the student goes to college. (To be sure, check with the plan administrator.) There is, however, a penalty if you try to use the money for other than educational expenses.

Some savings plans let you choose where your money is invested, so you can select a strategy that fits with your level of risk tolerance.

### Tax status of college savings plans

The tax rule is the same as it is for guaranteed tuition plans. No federal and state taxes are due on the yearly income that your account earns. When you withdraw the money to pay college expenses, the amount is taxed at the student's rate. Some states exempt this income from any state tax.

### Need formula treatment

If you have a college savings plan and apply for aid, the total value of the account is reported as a parent asset on the FAFSA and is subject to a maximum contribution rate of 5.6 percent. The amount taken out is considered to be student income. The need formula does not count the first $2,200 of student income. Fifty percent of any amount above 2,200 is expected to go towards educational expenses. This need treatment is not as severe as a guaranteed or prepaid tuition plan, but it is tougher than money held in general savings.

> *Insider's advice:* If you plan to be an aid applicant, a college savings plan is a better place to put your money than a guaranteed or prepaid tuition program. You should, however, compare all aspects of college savings to general savings before deciding where to put your money.

## General Savings

You can save the money as you would for any large future purchase with the intention (but not the obligation) of using the money for tuition. This is the most flexible of the college savings options, but it means that you have to exercise the discipline necessary to make sure the funds are used for college expenses.

Your investment choices are almost unlimited, but you will have to decide if you are comfortable setting up a plan on your own (when to start, how much to put aside, and where to put your money) or if you need professional advice.

If the investment decision is yours, you want to design a plan that balances a reasonable rate of return with security. Keep in mind that your money has to be available to spend on a specific date. You won't be able to wait for your stock in XYZ Company to rebound to its previous high.

The basic rule is to accept more risk over a longer time period, then become more conservative as the enrollment date approaches.

If you want to set up your own plan, the calculators mentioned on page 21 can help you develop a savings goal, and you can decide where to invest your money. But, if you think there is a chance you will apply for aid at a future date, *don't forget to deposit the money in the parents' name.*

If you are not comfortable with making your own investment decisions, you should get in touch with a Certified Financial Planner (see Chapter 9, pages 134–135, for more information on financial planners) or an adviser at a financial institution like Merrill Lynch, American Express, or Fidelity. In return for the fee the individual or company will receive for managing your money, they will work with you to develop a plan that meets your objectives.

Some financial services have software programs that make college cost and savings projections and also factor in the after-tax accumulation based on your tax bracket and program rules. Once you know your objective, a financial adviser can provide a sensible investment strategy.

### Tax status of general savings plans

A general savings plan has no special tax status as the law specifies for federal and state programs. How much you will pay in taxes on the interest earned each year as well as the amount taken out to pay for college depends on the type of investment and the tax bracket of the individual who owns the money.

> **Insider's Tip:** Of the three ways to save for college—guaranteed or prepaid tuition, college savings, and general savings—the need formula expects less from general savings in the parents' name than the other two. Depending on the amount you accumulate, the bottom-line difference among the three plans in how much a family is asked to contribute from their savings can be substantial.

## Need formula treatment

The value of the savings plan at the time your child applies for financial aid is reported on the FAFSA as either a parental or student asset, depending on whose name the money is held. If it is a parent asset, no more than 5.6 percent of the total is expected as a parental contribution. If the savings are owned by your child, 35 percent of the total is expected as a student contribution.

While parent assets placed in either a general savings or college savings plan have the same 5.6 percent maximum contribution rate, the amount you withdraw each year from the college savings plan is counted as student income. Money that you withdraw from general savings is not considered to be student income.

# SPONSORS OF GUARANTEED OR PREPAID TUITION AND COLLEGE SAVINGS PLANS

If you decide that a college-specific plan meets your needs better than a general savings program, you should know about the three main categories of such programs—federal, state, and private.

## Federal Plans

### Education IRA

If you are under the income limits ($110,000 for single filers, $160,000 for joint filers), you can contribute up to $500 per year per child. Payments are not tax deductible, but you do not pay taxes on yearly earnings and withdrawals. In the year in which you contribute to an Education IRA, you can not put money into another tax-free savings plan. In the year in which you withdraw money from an Education IRA, you can not claim a tuition tax credit. See Chapter 7, pages 113–114, for an explanation of tuition tax credits.

### Series EE bonds

You can purchase these bonds in denominations from $25 to $5,000, with a $15,000 limit per year. When your child attends college, you cash in the bonds to pay for education expenses. If used in this manner (you must hold the bond for five years), the interest earned on an EE bond does not count as part of your income. There is, however, an income limitation for you to receive this tax break. At the time you cash the bond, your income must be less than $68,100 if you are a single taxpayer or $109,650 if you file a joint tax return. These income limits are for 1999 and will increase in future years.

The advantage of the EE bond is security and, if your income is under the limit, tax-free appreciation. The disadvantage is a relatively low rate of return. For more information, call 202-377-7715.

### IRAs (Individual Retirement Arrangements)

There are two types of regular IRAs—deductible and Roth, or nondeductible. As the name implies, IRAs are intended for you to accumulate money for retirement. A deductible IRA means that you can subtract the amount you contribute from your income before you figure how much you owe in taxes. Contributions to a Roth IRA are made from after tax dollars—you cannot deduct the amount of your deposit.

I mention these two types of IRAs as possible college savings options since both plans allow you to withdraw money before age 59½ without incurring the usual 10 percent early withdrawal tax if the funds are used for education expenses.

## State Plans

These are referred to as 529 plans from the section of the Internal Revenue Code that defines their tax status. Approximately 45 states have or are developing a guaranteed or prepaid tuition plan, a college savings program, or both. Usually, you must be a state resident to be able to participate.

If you happen to live in a state that does not have its own plan, a number of states offer their plans without a residency restriction. You can read about eligibility requirements on the Internet site for a state's program.

### Where to get more information on the savings plan in your state

There is a helpful Internet site developed by the College Savings Plan Network in Lexington, Kentucky. It provides a link to the department within the state that operates the savings plan. There you will find information about what type of program is offered, an e-mail address, and a toll-free telephone number. Go to http://www.collegesavings.org/. Click on "Your State." Click on a map of the U.S. to select a state. Appendix A contains a list of the states with savings plans and their Web sites.

## Private Plans

### The CollegeSure Certificate of Deposit

This plan is offered by the College Savings Bank in New Jersey. You buy a CD with a rate of return equal to the percent increase in the College Board's Independent Colleges 500 Index—a college cost inflation indicator. The idea is that your money grows as fast as the costs of the average private college. Over the last ten years, the CollegeSure CD has averaged a 6 percent yield. The CDs are FDIC insured.

The College Savings Bank also offers a number of other savings plans, including traditional IRA, Education IRA, Roth IRA, and a special arrangement with the Montana program, which has no residency requirements or restrictions on where the student can attend college.

### Tuition Plan Consortium

The Tuition Plan Consortium (TPC) is a program developed by a group of more than 100 private colleges in response to state guaranteed tuition plans.

Participating colleges have formed a nonprofit corporation that is in the process of establishing a prepaid tuition program that would allow you to buy tuition shares that are later redeemable at any one of the member colleges.

The Tuition Plan Consortium has asked for a ruling that would give its depositors the same tax benefits that are currently enjoyed by those who participate in a state prepaid tuition plan. Information about the outcome of this request and other details of how the TPC program works will be posted on the *Insider's Guide* Internet site.

# A CHECKLIST FOR SAVERS

- ✔ If you have already put money aside, you should occasionally review where you stand in relation to your objectives.

- ✔ Are you getting a reasonable rate of return? The yearly growth should equal or exceed increases in college costs.

- ✔ How safe is your investment? As your child gets closer to college age, you want to make sure that the money will be there when you need it.

✔ If you are shooting for a dollar amount, how are you progressing? As your child begins to make a college list, are you purchasing the amount of tuition you had expected, or is an adjustment needed?

✔ If you have a monthly plan, have you been able to increase your contributions as your income has gone up? How does your likely accumulation compare to college costs?

✔ Do you have a reasonably good idea of whether or not you will be an aid applicant? If you think you might qualify for need aid, it is time to find out how the need formula will look at your savings. The basic rules can be found on pages 22–27 in this chapter, with updates provided on the *Insider's Guide* Internet site through http://www.petersons. com.

✔ Use one of the Internet calculators mentioned on page 21 in this chapter to enter what you have done so far, and revise your assumptions about your monthly contributions and rate of return.

For an update on college costs, go to http://www.collegequest. com. From the home page, click on "Pick," click on "Alphabetical List of Colleges," and enter the colleges for which you would like to see current costs.

## SUMMARY OF KEY POINTS

- Saving for college is a good idea, but be careful where you put your money.

- The sooner you start, the better off you are.

- Set a monthly savings goal and stick to it.

- Use an Internet savings calculator to do your figuring for you.

- Your savings strategy depends on whether or not you think you will be an aid applicant.

---◇---

## IF YOU WILL APPLY FOR AID

Put parents' money in the parents' name. Avoid guaranteed or prepaid tuition plans. Carefully weigh the advantages and disadvantages of college savings compared to general savings.

## IF YOU WILL NOT APPLY FOR AID

Since you don't have to worry about how the need formula deals with your savings, your investment decision can be based on security, rate of return, tax advantages, and whether or not there are restrictions on college attendance.

---◇---

# CHAPTER 3

# BEFORE YOU ENTER THE HIGHWAY: GETTING OFF TO A GOOD START

- Clearing up misconceptions
- The purpose of financial aid
- Why the numbers are important to you
- The truth about college costs
- The top financial aid Internet sites
- Summary of key points

The goal of the *Insider's Guide* is to make it easier for you to pay for the college education of your children. (If you are a part-time, adult, or graduate student, there is information about how to pay for your own education in Chapter 8, Side Roads: Nontraditional Students.)

This chapter is intended to set the stage for the chapters that follow. There is a tendency for authors of aid books to jump right into the detail about process and procedures. I don't know if financial aid is unique in this regard, but I often hear talk about aspects of student aid that is off the mark in one way or another. Sometimes the information that is passed along is not quite right—it may be incomplete or outdated. Other times, what families tell me is simply incorrect.

# CLEARING UP MISCONCEPTIONS

## The Poor Get All the Aid and the Rich Can Afford to Pay, Making It Tough for Middle-Income Families

My experience is that the so-called "middle-income squeeze" that you often hear about is more a state of mind than a reality. Families that feel the need formula asks for an unreasonably high contribution attribute their disappointment to their middle-class status. (I have heard families earning anywhere from $30,000 to $150,000 describe themselves as the squeezed middle class.)

The actual problem is not the income range in which you fall but the following three characteristics of need aid:

- The need formula assumes that paying for education should be the highest priority for spending discretionary income, and many families are not prepared philosophically or economically to deal with this fact.

- There is not enough available financial aid to meet every student's need. As a result, there often is a "gap" that causes families to have to stretch beyond their calculated contribution and come up with even more money.

- Since many of the federal and state grant programs are limited to lower-income families, there is a higher probability of receiving a student loan as part of the aid package.

## There Are Scholarships That Go Begging Each Year

In a sense, this statement is true. It is estimated that about $200 million in scholarships are unassigned in a given year. There are, however, two important points to keep in mind. First, the $200 million represents less than 1 percent of gift aid given out each year, a tiny sum compared to awarded scholarships and grants.

Second, scholarships go begging because they have such tight restrictions that it is difficult to find a qualified student. Here are the restrictions of actual scholarships. Do you qualify for any of these?

- Children of glassblowers

- Students named Hoolihan

- An Eagle Scout from St. Louis who attends Princeton University

To learn more about searching for scholarships, see Chapter 4, Reducing the Toll I: How to Find Scholarships.

## College Costs Are Out of Control

It is true that in the last decade, college costs have risen about twice as fast as the Consumer Price Index. Costs have also outpaced increases in family income. From an overall viewpoint, paying the college bill requires a greater sacrifice than it did years ago. There are, however, other considerations that make the picture less worrisome.

College costs have been increasing less than the rate of return on a typical investment. Families that put aside money for college can choose a prepaid tuition plan that is guaranteed to keep up with tuition increases. Other savings plans produce even higher rates of return. In our present economy, the best way to keep ahead of college cost increases in a well-thought-out savings plan.

Most colleges add money to their financial aid budgets when they increase costs. This means that while non-aid students pay more, many aid students have their awards increased to compensate for the higher costs. Although a college's tuition may increase by 5 percent or so, a family on a fixed income may not have to pay any more.

For more information about the college cost issue, see pages 41–43 in this chapter.

## I Am Penalized if I Save For College

If a family looks into various college savings options and chooses the right plan for them (while knowing how assets are treated in the need formula), they will find that only a small portion of their savings will be expected to go toward paying the college bill.

For more, see pages 22–27 in Chapter 2, Preparing For Your Trip: Start a Savings Plan.

## I Don't Trust the Federal Government to Keep My Free Application for Federal Student Aid (FAFSA) Information Confidential

The FAFSA instructions explain how the information you enter can be used. In addition to the U.S. Department of Education, the primary recipients are your state aid program and the colleges you listed.

For FAFSAs that are selected for verification, your information is compared to IRS, Social Security, Selective Service, Immigration and Naturalization, and Veterans Administration databases. If you are involved in litigation, your information may be used as evidence in that process.

It is up to you to decide if these possible data exchanges invade your privacy. Remember, however, that the only means of access to about $52 billion of financial aid is through the FAFSA.

## Financial Aid Is a Negotiating Process

The majority of our nation's approximately 2,000 four-year colleges give you all the aid for which you qualify when they send you an award letter. No matter how good a student your child is or how persuasive your argument that you need more aid, there simply is not any additional money.

When negotiating is a possibility, it occurs most often at private colleges that have their own scholarships and grants. Some colleges (although not very many) actively solicit "appeals" (the financial aid term for negotiation) because they want the opportunity to match another college's award or otherwise increase an aid package to a more satisfactory level. These colleges are usually "enrollment sensitive"— they find themselves hard pressed to fill their freshman class with the number and type of students they need.

More common are colleges that are open to discussions with families about the terms of an award but don't encourage appeals. Your chance of negotiating successfully with these colleges depend on the merits of your case and whether the college has already spent its financial aid budget.

For more information, see pages 102–104 in Chapter 6, Choosing a Destination: The Role of Aid in Selecting a College.

### We Don't Make Much Money, So We Can't Afford an Expensive College

Our country's strong commitment to need-based aid is specifically targeted at proving this statement false. Each year, approximately $52 billion is awarded to students to lower the price they pay for college to an affordable level. The need system may not work perfectly, but you should trust it enough to apply to the colleges you want to attend. It then is a matter of completing the FAFSA and keeping your fingers crossed that you will receive an adequate aid package.

### Financial Aid Is So Complicated that I Need to Pay for Good Advice

I generally agree with the first part of this statement that financial aid is complicated. (After all, I wrote the *Insider's Guide* so you can better understand the process.)

However, I disagree with the idea that you should have to pay a substantial fee for guidance. Large fees (usually $100 or more) are charged by some scholarship search firms and financial aid "consultants." These businesses promise to find you money that you could not locate on your own. I advise against paying for such services until you have exhausted all the free advice that is available. If you reach the point where you feel you need more help, you should thoroughly check the credentials of the financial aid services company before you sign a contract.

For more on this subject, see pages 132–135 in Chapter 9, If You Still Have Questions.

## THE PURPOSE OF FINANCIAL AID

There is a lot at stake in selecting a college. As a parent, I'm sure you would like to see your son or daughter enroll at a college that best fits with your child's academic ability, extracurricular talents, and social values, but a college education costs money. Today, four years of college can have a "sticker price" of anywhere from $20,000 to $120,000.

If everyone had to pay the full price, it would be a matter of matching your child with a college you can afford. While this would simplify the college-going process, it would result in a very unfortunate outcome for American society. Students would be sorted among colleges based on income. Low-income students would attend the most inexpensive colleges (or none at all), middle-income students would attend the local public institution, and on up, so that only the wealthiest students would enroll at the high-cost colleges.

Fortunately for our country, there is a large amount of money available to provide discounts from the published cost. This money is called college financial aid, or student aid. To facilitate opportunity based on ability and not income, the U.S. has constructed by far the largest student aid program in the world—giving out about $65 billion in the most recent year.

Fewer than one out of four students actually pay the cost of college from their own income and assets. The remainder use a portion of this $65 billion discount program to lower their out-of-pocket expense.

———————————— ◇ ————————————

## FINANCIAL AID BY THE NUMBERS

The $65 billion that was available in 1997–98 (the most recent year available) can be looked at in different ways.

### Where it comes from:

- The federal government ..............................$44.0 billion
- States ......................................................$3.5 billion
- Colleges ................................................$11.2 billion
- Private sources.........................................$6.3 billion
  - $65.0 billion

## What kind of aid:

- Grants and scholarships .............................$28.0 billion

- Loans ....................................................$35.0 billion

- Work-study...............................................$2.0 billion
  - $65.0 billion

## Based on a needs test:

- Need......................................................$51.5 billion
- Non-need or merit ....................................$13.5 billion
  - $65.0 billion

*Note:* These figures, including both undergraduate and graduate aid and parental as well as student borrowing, are based on "Trends in Student Aid" published by the College Board. However, since their research did not include private scholarships, I have made an estimate of that category and added it to their data.

———————————— ◇ ————————————

# WHY THE NUMBERS ARE IMPORTANT TO YOU

### 80% of Aid is Awarded to Students Who Demonstrate Need

This figure is a surprise to many families I talk with. To them, financial aid means scholarships based on merit or performance. They think that to win a scholarship, you have to be an excellent student or a top athlete. If your child is neither, it becomes necessary to go on a search for scholarships. Since need rather than merit is the primary standard, it is important to read Chapter 5, Reducing the Toll II: How to Find Grants and Other Need Aid.

> *Insider's advice:* Unless you are absolutely sure you will not qualify for need aid, you should enter your family financial information in an Expected Family Contribution (EFC) estimator and compare it to likely college costs before you decide whether or not to apply for aid. This process is explained on pages 76–77 in Chapter 5, Reducing the Toll II: How to Find Grants and Other Need Aid.

### 54% of Aid Is in the Form of Loans

Don't think that financial aid consists only of scholarships or grants. The chances are that more than one half of the aid you receive will be a student loan. (Work-study jobs are also considered aid. When jobs are added to loans, 58 percent of aid is nonscholarship.)

### 68% of the Yearly Amount Is Funded by the Federal Government

Because there is federal aid in almost every award, Congress and the U. S. Department of Education control the process. They design the FAFSA, develop the need formula, and set most of the financial aid rules and regulations.

In return for the government's generosity, be prepared to be a small part of a very large computer-driven operation that processes 7 million applications each year. It is therefore important for you to follow instructions and meet deadlines. When complications do arise, the Department of Education tries to help through customer service phone lines. These numbers are listed in Chapter 9, If You Still Have Questions, on page 130.

### Only 8% of Aid Is in Merit Scholarships

Considering all the money in need-based grants, loans, and work-study, this is a relatively small piece of the pie, but it still adds up to $5 billion. It is therefore worthwhile to spend some time looking for these scholarships. I cover this subject in Chapter 4, Reducing the Toll I: How to Find Scholarships.

### What Works for Getting Admitted Also Works for Winning Scholarships

A financial aid strategy is to do the best you can inside and outside of the classroom. The level of academic and nonacademic performance you will need to be admitted to the colleges on your list is usually the standard used to award scholarships (assuming you meet the restrictions). This can also hold true for the amount of need-based grant in an aid package.

# THE TRUTH ABOUT COLLEGE COSTS

The public's view is that college is expensive and getting even more expensive. As a result, when families are questioned about their concerns for the future, they report that one of their primary worries is that they won't be able to afford to pay for the college education of their children.

The truth about the present state of college costs is that an argument can be made on either side of the issue. Some say that the cost of a college education remains a bargain and a good investment, while others cite recent cost increases as excessive.

### The "Costs Are Too High" Argument

The primary example that supports this opinion is how rapidly the cost of a college education has risen in the 1980s compared to inflation. Here are some of the facts.

- Seventy-one percent of those surveyed in a recent poll believe that college is too expensive.

- Since 1980–81, both public and private four-year college tuitions have increased more than 100 percent over inflation.

- During the same period, the median family income increased by only 12 percent, and low- and middle-income families saw very little of this increase.

- In the last eighteen years, only medical costs have risen at a more rapid rate than college costs.

Another attention-grabbing statistic about the expense of a college education is what it costs to attend a selective private college. In 1998–99 the average cost of tuition, room, and board for one of these colleges was about $30,000. If your child entered in the fall of 1999, you can expect to pay about $135,000 for four years, and this does not include books and personal expenses.

## The "College Is a Good Value" Argument

There are a number of points made in defense of the amount colleges charge for tuition. These include:

- Families greatly overestimate how much college actually costs. In a recent survey conducted by the American Council on Education, respondents gave the following estimates:

|  | Estimated cost of tuition | Actual cost of tuition |
|---|---|---|
| Community college | $4,026 | $1,239 |
| Four-year public (in-state) | $9,694 | $2,848 |
| Four-year private | $17,897 | $12,243 |

- The high costs of a college education that are most often cited are for the selective private institutions. The large majority of students attend public institutions with low tuitions. Almost three quarters of the students attending four-year institutions pay less than $8,000 in tuition. More than half pay less than $4,000.

- When financial aid is factored in, students only pay about 60 percent of the total budget.

- Due to state higher education subsidies, every student who attends a public college receives a large scholarship unrelated to financial need.

- Whatever you actually end up paying for college, it is a good investment. Over the course of a lifetime, compared to someone with only a high school diploma, a person with a B.A. degree is expected to earn about $800,000 more and those with advanced degrees, up to $2,200,000 more.

## My View on the Cost Issue

- Those who set tuitions have been somewhat slow to recognize the public's concern about college costs and are now paying attention and taking reasonable steps to hold down increases.

- The low tuitions of our public universities are one of the best buys in American higher education.

- For those who can't afford to pay the full cost, there are $65 billion in discounts available each year. The problem is that when you are deciding where to apply to college, it is easy to determine the sticker price but hard to figure out how much of a discount you might receive through the financial aid system. The lack of good financial aid information at an early point can cause you to limit your college choices more than you should. This is why I recommend that you use an EFC estimator early in the financial aid process. With an EFC figure in mind, you can do your college shopping with some idea of the price you might pay rather than concentrating on the sticker price.

- The way to deal with the fact that college costs are likely to continue to rise faster than inflation is to invest money in a college savings plan where your return is at least equal to increases in college costs. In the current economic climate, this is relatively easy to do. In fact, a number of the college savings options mentioned in Chapter 2, Preparing For Your Trip: Start a Savings Plan, guarantee such a rate of return.

A good Internet reference to find out the cost of any college you are interested in is http://www.collegequest.com. From the home page, go to "Pick," click on "Alphabetical Look-up," enter a college, and click on the college to go to a page that will show the cost.

# THE TOP FINANCIAL AID INTERNET SITES

There are many Web sites that contain financial aid information, but most of them treat paying for college as a topic under personal money management. There are relatively few Internet sites whose primary subject matter (sometimes combined with admission information) is financial aid. The best of these are:

**1. http://www.finaid.org** This is the granddaddy of them all. This was the first Web site devoted exclusively to financial aid. It is a very good site made even better by a recent redesign and expansion of topics.

Its main features include

- Loans
- Scholarships
- Other Types of Aid
- Financial Aid Applications
- Answering Your Questions
- Calculators
- Beyond Financial Aid
- About Financial Aid
- Students
- Parents
- Educators
- Key Word Search

**2. http://www.collegequest.com** This is a comprehensive Web site, developed by Peterson's, designed as "one-stop shopping" for the college-going student, so it contains both admission and financial aid information. Financial aid is one of six main subject areas. The others are Personal Organizer, Prepare, Pick, eApply, and Idea Exchange.

To use the site, it is necessary to register as a member. Most of the information is free, but you can elect to subscribe to

CollegeQuest Plus, a fee-based service that provides additional information not usually available on other admission and financial aid sites.

Under Financial Aid, CollegeQuest's main features are

- Saving for College
- Preparing for the Financial Aid Process
- Applying for and Receiving Financial Aid
- Understanding Financial Aid
- Entering the Need-Based System
- Searching for Scholarships and Awards
- Comparing and Evaluating Awards
- Paying the College Bill

Within the Idea Exchange is a section called Ask the Expert, where you can ask financial aid questions.

**3. http://www.collegeboard.org** The College Board site is similar to CollegeQuest, as it includes both admission and financial aid subject matter. Also, since the College Board is an association of high school and college members that sponsors the SAT, Advanced Placement exams, and financial aid PROFILE, it offers families access to its various services through Internet registration.

Under Financial Aid Services, its main features are

- CSS/Financial Aid PROFILE
- Scholarship Search
- College Costs
- Financial Aid Facts
- College Credit Loans
- EFC Calculator
- Financial Aid Calculators
- College Credit Tip Sheets

**4. http://www.salliemae.com** Sallie Mae (the name comes from Student Loan Marketing Association) is a large financial services company that specializes in higher education. Its main business is funding and collecting student loans.

If you go to Students/Families and then High School Student, you will find

- Paying For College
- How to pay for college
- Calculating aid eligibility
- Financial aid time line
- Applying for financial aid
- Understanding aid awards
- Financial Aid Tools
- Financial aid calculators, including CollegeCalc software that is downloadable so you can run calculators without a live Internet connection
- Top 10 financial aid shopping tips
- CASHE Online Scholarship Service
- Planning For College
- Saving for college
- Ask College Answer

**5. http://www.ed.gov/fin aid**. Developed by the U.S. Department of Education, this is the main site that explains the federal government's need-based student assistance programs (also called Title IV aid).

Under Financial Aid for Students you will find

- What's New
- Finding Out About Financial Aid
- Applying for Federal Student Aid
- Paying Back Your Student Loan

- Customer Feedback

This Web site also shows various ways to file the FAFSA.

There is another Internet site that approaches paying for college from the viewpoint of parents. The organization is called College Parents of America, and the site is located at http://www.collegeparents.org. In addition to money matters, there is information on academic and social issues that are of interest to parents.

## SUMMARY OF KEY POINTS

- Aid is too important to act on what your friend or neighbor tells you. Get your information from a reliable source.

- There is a lot of financial aid available each year, but the total is not what is important to you. You need to know which piece you might be eligible for and how to go about getting it.

- Need aid (grants, subsidized loans, and work-study) and not merit scholarships is where 80 percent of the money is. It pays to check your need aid eligibility.

- College costs have risen faster than inflation (and probably will continue to do so), but the rewards of a college degree have never been greater.

- There are a number of very good financial aid Internet sites that can supply information, search for scholarships, and help you apply for aid. Nearly all of these services are free.

# CHAPTER 4

# REDUCING THE TOLL I: HOW TO FIND SCHOLARSHIPS

---

- Education benefits
- Where to look for scholarships
- Take a personal inventory
- Further comments on scholarships
- Summary of key points

---

It's now time to enter the financial aid process.

Hopefully, you started a savings plan a number of years ago, and your child has done well in a precollege academic curriculum and exhibits the type of personal qualities and talents that will make him or her a strong candidate for admission and receiving gift aid.

This chapter deals with scholarships. Chapter 5, Paying the Toll II: Applying for Grants and Other Need Aid, covers grants, as well as student loans and work study, in detail.

## WORKING DEFINITIONS

### ✔Gift aid

Free money that doesn't have to be repaid. It includes scholarships, education benefits, and grants.

### ✔Scholarship

Gift aid that does not have a needs test. A scholarship, or merit aid, is usually awarded based on talent exhibited by the student. Since a competition is involved, a student is said to "win" a scholarship. Examples are the National Merit Scholarship, the Intel Science Talent Search, and athletic scholarships.

As used in the *Insider's Guide*, a scholarship means free money that does not require a demonstration of need.

### ✔Education benefit

This is another category of non-need gift aid. Education benefits are not won but are given because of an attribute of the student or parent. Examples are GI Bill benefits and tuition remission payments paid by an employer on behalf of an employee.

### ✔Grant

Gift aid that is based on need. Students are "awarded" grants. Examples are the Federal Pell Grant and state grants. Chapter 5 covers grants, as well as student loans and work study.

To summarize: Gift aid without a need test is either an **education benefit** or a **scholarship**. Gift aid that requires a demonstration of need is a **grant**.

———————————— ◇ ————————————

# EDUCATION BENEFITS

Let's first look at education benefits. This money is automatic—if you meet the eligibility standards, you receive the funds without having to enter a competition or demonstrate need.

You usually do not have to search for these funds. It is in the interest of the sponsoring organization or the employer to publicize the education benefit that it offers. In fact, the existence of an education benefit is often highlighted in recruiting efforts for new workers. Education benefits can come to you as a result of where you are employed or through a relationship with someone who has died or become disabled (called survivor benefits).

## Work-Related Education Benefits

The availability of an education benefit is usually known beforehand to prospective workers. Two of the largest providers, the military and Americorps, advertise the education benefit they provide in their recruiting literature.

***Insider's advice:*** Your strategy to receive an education benefit is straightforward. You (parents or student) decide if you want to work for the organization, college, or company that offers such a benefit.

### The GI Bill

The largest education benefit program comes from joining the military. In return for serving, you will receive payments under the GI Bill (now called the **Montgomery GI Bill**). See Chapter 8, Side Roads: Nontraditional Students, on page 125, for more information.

The Veterans Administration Web site has full details about GI Bill benefits at http://www.va.gov/education/C30.htm/.

### Americorps

If you serve in Americorps, a federal program that provides services to communities in need, you will receive an education benefit of $4,725 per year for two years in addition to a living allowance and medical coverage. The $4,725 benefit is restricted to paying off future or existing student loans.

A possible strategy is to serve in Americorps between high school and college (there is a minimum age of 18) and hold the education benefit in reserve for the time when you are given a loan. As a practical matter, however, nearly all Americorps workers join after they graduate from college and use the education benefit to reduce their prior student loan.

The Americorps Web site at http://www.cns.gov/americorps/ has stories of individual participants in the program and detailed information about this community service benefit program.

### Private employers

The existence of nongovernment education benefits is somewhat harder to track down. There are a number of corporations and colleges that offer tuition assistance as part of the company's overall benefit package.

---

*Insider's advice:* A possible parental strategy is to look into employment with a college or company that has a tuition reimbursement plan. You should check with the colleges, nonprofit corporations, and large companies in your local area to see if their employment benefit packages include tuition remission.

While this tactic may be impractical for the main wage earner, it could be a consideration as the person with the secondary income looks at potential employers. Keep in mind that a tax-free tuition benefit of $10,000 is equivalent to about $15,000 in additional salary (assuming a 33 percent tax bracket).

Since colleges or corporations usually have a minimum length of service requirement to receive a tuition benefit, this strategy should be pursued before your child's senior year in high school if you want to qualify for the benefit for all four undergraduate years.

---

## Survivor Benefits

### Social Security

If one of your parents is disabled or deceased, the survivors receive benefits. The money paid to children ends at age 18 unless they are enrolled in college. Otherwise, benefits continue to age 21. The only strategy involved here is to be aware of this provision and to make sure you verify college enrollment so the benefits continue to be paid. The Social Security Administration's general Web site is http://www.ssa. gov/.

### State programs

A number of states give education benefits to the children of police officers and fire fighters who were killed or permanently disabled in the line of duty. States also give awards to the children of members of the military who were permanently disabled, killed, or reported missing in action. State agencies responsible for higher education and state departments of veterans affairs can provide information about these programs. Lists of these agencies can be found in Appendix B.

# WHERE TO LOOK FOR SCHOLARSHIPS

### Setting the Record Straight

Before you read about searching for scholarships, you should keep in mind that scholarships are hard to get. Most of them are quite competitive and require a high level of ability in the area in which the scholarship is offered. (The major exception to the "highly competitive" statement is a number of state scholarships given to students with a B average or higher.)

While many families understand the competitiveness of a "name brand" scholarship like the National Merit award, there is a feeling that there are a number of "easy to get" scholarships out there if only they could be found. The idea that scholarships are like ripe fruit ready to be picked has been advanced by fee-based search companies that say they will locate such scholarships for you.

There are, in fact, very few such scholarships. But if you want to look for them (along with more well-known awards), the free scholarship databases are as comprehensive as fee-based searches.

## The Internet

Using the Internet is the primary method for locating private scholarships. (By "private," I mean awards other than federal, state, or college.) These are the types of scholarships a family usually thinks about when they want to know where to look for a scholarship.

The Internet method is the most efficient in searching for scholarships. The computer does the matching job for you, and then, if you decide to apply for a scholarship, the program will format a letter of application. Another advantage of an Internet search is its timeliness—the scholarship information can be updated continuously rather than on the yearly cycle that is common in print publications.

***Insider's advice:*** It doesn't hurt to try a couple of the free Internet scholarship searches. You may find a few scholarships that look interesting and worth applying for, but don't expect too much. I have yet to see a scholarship search organization publish a report on the success rate for students who apply for awards contained in their database. My guess is that the "hit rate" is very small and the large majority of users don't receive any aid through the search process.

Scholarship searches should only be done in addition to applying for federal, state, and college scholarships, the most likely source of assistance for the typical student. Also, as described in Chapter 5, Reducing the Toll II: How to Look for Grants and Other Need Aid, you should use an Expected Family Contribution (EFC) estimator on the Internet to determine your chances of receiving need aid.

### Scholarship search Web sites

Here is a list of sites that provide free scholarship searches. All of them have links under "Scholarships" at http://www.finaid.com. If you want to go to any of the sites directly, I have also indicated their addresses.

- **Peterson's CollegeQuest**

*Register, click on "Financial Aid," click on "Applying For and Receiving Financial Aid," click on "Searching For Scholarships and Awards," go to "Current Sub-section," and click on "Scholarship and Award Search."*

http://www.CollegeQuest.com

- **College Board**

*Click on "Students and Parents," under "Searches," click on "Scholarships."*

http://www.collegeboard.com

- **FastWEB**

*Register, go to "Scholarship Search."*

http://www.fastweb.com

- **Wintergreen/Orchard House**

*Click on "Scholarship Search."*

http://www.collegenet.com/mach25/

- **SRN Express**

*Complete the scholarship search form.*

http://www.rams.com/srn/execsearch.htm

- **Sallie Mae**

*Click on "Scholarship Search."*

http://scholarships.salliemae.com

> **Insider's Advice:** Since the free scholarship search services contain essentially the same listings of awards as those that you pay for, I don't recommend you pay a fee.
>
> Unfortunately, the business of charging a family money to help locate financial aid has attracted a number of rip-off artists who charge high fees and give little in return. Scholarship scams are an area about which the Federal Trade Commission receives many complaints. The Internet site http://www.finaid.org has additional information under "common scholarship scams."

## Publications

Consulting a scholarship reference book remains a reliable method for looking for scholarships. Although more labor intensive than using the Internet, the ability to browse through a book gives you a good feel for the larger scholarship picture.

Scholarship reference books are readily available, most likely for free in your high school guidance office or public library. Commercial bookstores have a number of guides in their college section. When you find a scholarship that relates to your attributes and qualifications, make a list of the address and write for an application.

──────────── ◇ ────────────

## EXAMPLES OF LARGE PRIVATE SCHOLARSHIPS

Each year, *Peterson's Scholarships, Grants & Prizes* provides a complete directory of private scholarships and grants. In 1999–2000, these scholarship programs provided the highest top individual awards:

- The Raissa Tselentis Memorial Johann Sebastian Bach International Solo Recital Competitions ............$130,000

- The Margaret Fairbank Jory Copying Assistance (musical composition) Program........................................$70,000

- The Intel Science Talent Search ............................$50,000
- Monopoly Game at McDonald's .........................$50,000
- Scholarships for Blind Jewish Community Professionals (for rabbis, cantors, and Jewish community workers) .........................................................$50,000
- North Carolina Police Corps Scholarships (for future police officers) .................................................$40,000
- Lutheran Seminary Awards..............................$39,000

———————————— ◇ ————————————

## High School Guidance Offices

For large national scholarships, your high school guidance office and sometimes the public library will receive and make available to you information from the program sponsors. Examples of these types of awards are the National Merit, Coca-Cola, and Intel Science Scholarships.

For local scholarships, like American Legion, Rotary, and Parent Teachers Association, once again, your high school guidance office is probably the best source, but you may also find announcements in the town newspaper or public library.

## Federal Programs

The federal government concentrates nearly all of its student aid efforts on loans and need-based grants. The main exceptions are scholarships and benefits that are related to military service. The primary benefit program is the Montgomery GI Bill, as described in Chapter 8, page 125. Scholarships are either Reserve Officer Training Corps (ROTC) tuition payments or a free education at a military service academy. Information about these opportunities can be found on pages 64–65.

The federal government does support one large nonmilitary scholarship—the Robert C. Byrd Honors Scholarship Program. See page 63 for details.

### State Scholarship Agencies

Nearly every state sponsors an academic scholarship program. To learn more about the eligibility rules for the academic scholarships in your state, go to Internet site http://nassgap.org. This is the site of the National Association of State Grant and Aid Programs. The association provides links to the department that gives scholarships in thirty-four states. A full list of state agencies and their Web sites can be found in Appendix A.

### Colleges

Colleges are one of the largest sources of scholarships.

Most college merit scholarships are primarily academic awards, with character and leadership as secondary factors. A college's admission material will usually spell out the standards.

Carefully read the scholarship information for all the colleges on your list. In general, college scholarships are of two types.

- Regular merit awards, with the amount based on the rating that the admission office gives to your application.

- Restricted (or "named") scholarships that often take into account other attributes beyond your academic record.

> *Insider's advice:* Once you find out about the requirements for the scholarships at your colleges, start to build your credentials in a way that improves your chances of winning one of the awards.

## TAKE A PERSONAL INVENTORY

You should be prepared before you start your scholarship search. Make a list of your personal attributes, academic record, talents, work experience, and affiliations. Do the same for your parents—employer, membership in organizations, and military connections.

As a guide for making your list, here are the main categories in which scholarships are awarded:

- Personal characteristics

- General academic

- Academic subject area or career related

- Talent, including athletics

- School activities

- Employment or volunteer work

- Activities and organizations outside of school

- Religious affiliation

- Prior military service

*The last four categories—employment or volunteer work, activities and organizations outside of school, religious affiliation, and prior military service—can be based on the attributes of either the parent or the student.*

## Personal Characteristics

For the most part, this category consists of permanent attributes, although some may be changed. Examples of personal characteristics that are also scholarship eligibility standards are age, gender, citizenship, year in college, religion, ethnicity, heritage, disability, and state of residence.

### Special categories

*Disabilities*

The American Council on Education (ACE) in Washington, D.C., serves as the clearinghouse for information about aid for students with disabilities. Under the sponsorship of ACE is the HEATH Resource Center that publishes "Financial Aid for Students with Disabilities." Further information can be found on the Internet by going to http://www.acenet.edu and clicking on "Information from HEATH" under "New Resources."

It may also be worthwhile to check directly with an organization that supports people with a specific disability, such as the American Council for the Blind or the vocational rehabilitation office in your state.

*Members of minority groups*

There are many scholarship opportunities for minority students—mainly the affirmative action categories of African American, Hispanic, or Native American. Although not as plentiful, there are also scholarships for Asian-American students. Students who are members of minority groups should remember the following important points:

1. You should realize that a minority student can compete for any generally available scholarship. You don't have to limit yourself to minority awards.

2. Keep in mind that the most common scholarship restriction is that the scholarship is for minority students, meaning any of the above three categories.

3. There are scholarships for specific minority groups, like the Jackie Robinson Scholarship, the National Hispanic Scholarship, the Japanese American Citizens League Awards, and the Cherokee Nation scholarship.

When you go to the Internet site for one of the free scholarship searches mentioned earlier in this chapter and indicate your minority status, you will receive a list of scholarships with that particular restriction. Other Internet sites that contain information about minority scholarships are the National Action Council for Minorities in Engineering at http://www.nacme.org, the Hispanic Scholarship Fund at http://www.hsfnet/scholarship, and MOLIS Scholarship Search at http://www.fie.com/molis/scholar.htm.

---  ◇  ---

# Ron Brown Scholar Program

This is a national program of scholarships for academically talented African-American high school seniors who show traits of leadership, commitment to public service, and desire to make a difference. In addition, applicants must demonstrate financial need. Information about this exceptionally well-funded scholarship program can be found at http://www.ronbrown.org.

---  ◇  ---

Two books that have aid listings for minority students are *Minority Financial Aid Directory,* by Lemuel Berry Jr., and *Directory of Financial Aids for Minorities,* by Gail Ann Schlachter and R. David Webber.

Scholarships for Native Americans usually come from either the local tribe or the U.S. Department of Indian Affairs. If you are a Native American (usually defined as at least one-fourth Native American blood), you will find about 100 award sources in a typical scholarship search database, including many tribal scholarships.

The U.S. Bureau of Indian Affairs is the largest sponsor of scholarships for Native Americans. Check with the local BIA agency or your tribal office for more information. The U.S. Bureau of Indian Affairs Web site is http://www.doi.gov/bureau-indian-affairs.html.

All students who are members of minority groups should carefully read the financial aid information of the colleges on their list, available either through the Internet home page or in printed material. Any special awards for minorities will be described.

*Women students*

If you are female, it is unlikely that your gender will be a factor when it comes to competing for a scholarship. As far as I know, there are no federal or state scholarships with such a qualification. There are state scholarships for traditionally women's occupations, such as nurse training. Similarly, except for women's colleges, it is unusual for a college to use gender as an eligibility standard for awarding its own money.

You will, however, find a number of private gender-based awards in a scholarship search database. These include awards given by women's organizations like Girls Incorporated, Big Sister, and Junior Miss. It is also common for sponsors in occupations where women are traditionally underrepresented to offer scholarships. Examples are scholarships for women in accounting, architecture, engineering, and construction.

## General Academic

The strength of your overall academic record is a factor in most scholarships. The indicators are grade point average (GPA), class rank, and results on standardized tests—either the SAT I or ACT.

Your scholarship preparation is the same as it would be if you are planning to apply to a selective college—choose a strong curriculum and try for the highest grades and test scores. In most cases, scholarship competitions do not have specific academic requirements, so you should do the best you can and keep your fingers crossed. Some scholarships, however, are awarded based on published standards. It is important that you learn about any of these "entitlement" scholarships for which you might be eligible.

### Entitlement scholarships

Entitlement scholarships are given automatically if you meet the standard. A number of state academic scholarships are set up like this. An example is the ***Florida Bright Futures Scholarship*** program. If you have a B average and 3.2 GPA, you receive $1,500. A 3.5 GPA or higher gets you $2,000. With entitlement awards, your scholarship strategy is obvious—shoot for grades that are above the cut-off points. For information about the academic scholarship program in your state, check with your state higher education agency, which is listed in Appendix A.

---◇---

## ROBERT C. BYRD HONORS SCHOLARSHIP PROGRAM

Byrd Scholarships are academically based awards to outstanding high school graduates. Although funds come from the federal government, each state department of elementary and secondary education administers the scholarship program, setting the specific rules on who qualifies for the scholarships and how the money is distributed. A file of all state elementary-secondary education agencies with hyperlinks can be found at http://www.ed.gov /offices/OPE/agencies.html.

---◇---

### Academic Subject Area or Career Related

These are scholarships based on accomplishments in a field of study, like engineering, or a single subject, like biology, American history, or creative writing.

There are many scholarships sponsored by organizations and companies that are looking to support students who will eventually pursue a career in the field they represent. Examples are the National Association of Public Accountants, the American Institute of Architects, and the American Chemical Society.

---◇---

## SCHOLARSHIPS IN SUBJECT AREAS AND CAREER FIELDS

In 1999–2000, in Peterson's Non-Institutional Aid Database, one of the largest databases of private aid, slightly more than 50 percent of more than 3,000 programs are awarded on the basis of a student's planned area of academic subject area or career field. Of the categories with more than one percent of the award programs in the database, this is how they rank:

**The top five fields:** Health and Medical Sciences (10%), Engineering/Technology (6%), Nursing (4.5%), Social Sciences (4%), Agriculture (3.8%)

**2.5 percent to 3 percent:** Biology, Business/Consumer Services, Communications, Education, Journalism, Physical Sciences and Mathematics

**2 percent to 2.4 percent:** Applied Sciences, Food Science/Nutrition, Humanities, Performing Arts

**1.5 percent to 1.9 percent:** Agribusiness, Animal/Veterinary Sciences, Computer Science/Data Processing, Dental Health/Services, Earth Science, Law/Legal Services, Library Sciences, Natural Resources, Therapy/Rehabilitation

**1 percent to 1.5 percent:** Area/Ethnic Studies, Arts, Aviation/Aerospace, Chemical Engineering, Civil Engineering, Electrical/Electronic Engineering, Engineering-Related Technologies, History, Home Economics, Horticulture/Floriculture, Mechanical Engineering, Travel/Tourism, TV/Radio Broadcasting

––––––––––––––––––  ◇  ––––––––––––––––––

> ***Insider's advice:*** Perform well at the highest level courses you can take in your strongest subject. Extra efforts, like participating in competitions and finding summer work in your subject area, add to your credentials and make you a better candidate.

### ROTC/Service academies

While your future career is probably the farthest thing from your mind right now, one possibility you should think about is whether or not you see yourself serving in the military as an officer. There are millions of dollars in scholarships given each year to students who attend one of the military service academies (Army, Navy, Air Force, or Coast Guard) or who join the Reserve Officer Training Corps (ROTC) on a college campus. Here are the Web sites for the military service academies:

- **United States Military Academy:** http://www.usma.edu
- **United States Naval Academy:** http://www.nadn.navy.mil/

- **United States Air Force Academy:** http://www.usafa.edu

- **United States Coast Guard Academy:** http://www.cga.edu

The Air Force, the Navy (which, in respect to ROTC, includes the Marines), and the Army each run a different ROTC program. Here are their central Web sites:

- **Air Force:** http://www.usarotc.com

- **Army:** http://www.afoats.af.mil/rotc.htm

- **Navy/Marines:** http://www.cnet.navy.mil/nrotc/nrotc.htm

ROTC units at particular colleges and universities frequently have their own page within the general college Web site.

If you are seriously considering becoming an officer, preparation is important. Review your curriculum to make sure you are taking the proper courses. You also should participate in sports and seek leadership roles in various activities. If your high school has a Junior ROTC unit, you should join it.

## Talent

Scholarships given to top-notch athletes are one large subcategory. In addition, colleges and private scholarship sponsors make awards to students who perform well in a variety of other fields, such as theater, dance, music, art, and writing.

In 1999–2000, slightly more than 33 percent of scholarship programs in Peterson's Non-Institutional Aid Database were awarded for a talent.

### Athletics

Although athletic scholarships are probably the most publicized form of financial aid, they are also among the hardest to win. There are thousands of good high school athletes, but only a small fraction will eventually receive a full award.

As a general rule (there are exceptions), athletic scholarships do not go to the merely good athlete but to a player at the elite level. A good athlete might be an all-league or all-county performer. An elite athlete probably has been named to an all-state, all-region, or all-American team.

Furthermore, there are not that many full scholarships given out. In most minor sports (everything but football and basketball), coaches usually award "partials," meaning one-half tuition or less. Also keep in mind that not all colleges give athletic scholarships. Neither the Ivy League nor NCAA Division III colleges grant athletic awards.

***Insider's Advice:*** Concentrate on your best sport, seek good coaching, and play at the highest level, including the best out-of-school competition you can find. Since coaches recruit nationally, they often cannot see a prospective recruit in person. Once you've established yourself as an outstanding athlete, it is very important that you present yourself in the best light. A good videotape of you in a strong performance can be the difference between winning a scholarship or not.

You should contact the coach of your sport at the colleges you are interested in. If you are just starting your college search process, there are guidebooks, such as *Peterson's Sports and Athletic Scholarships,* which list colleges by their NCAA division, show the sports in which they offer athletic scholarships, and provide names and addresses of specific coaches.

The NCAA has a Web site (http://www.ncaa.org) that has, among other information, all the basic rules that a prospective student athlete needs to know about the all-important and potentially disruptive issues related to maintaining eligibility for a sports scholarship.

***A Note to Women Athletes:*** With the expansion of women's teams under Title IX of the Higher Education Act, there are more and more opportunities for women to win athletic scholarships. At the same time, compared to male athletes, there are fewer women playing some of these sports at the highest level. (Some examples are lacrosse, ice hockey, crew and, to some extent, field hockey and soccer.) If you are an outstanding woman athlete, keep at it and follow the advice given above. When it comes to supply and demand, you are in a much better position to win an athletic scholarship than a male athlete.

## Other talents

Athletic awards are not the only talent-based scholarships. There are many scholarships given to students who excel in music, theater, art, dance, writing, debate, and so forth. This category is usually closely connected to school activities, since most students exhibit their talent through their high school.

*Insider's Advice:* The approach you should take in preparing yourself to possibly win a scholarship is similar to the one I pointed out in the previous section on athletic scholarships. There are many students who are very good within the context of their high school setting. But this level alone is often not enough to compete regionally or statewide for a scholarship. Do all you can to improve your talent so you are among the best within your county, state, or region. If you have a talent, strive to improve it to such a level that a college will value your accomplishments enough to give you a scholarship.

## School Activities

In the pursuit of good grades, this is an area that is sometimes overlooked. A strong record—this means *noteworthy accomplishments in important activities,* not merely a long list of club memberships—builds a record that will help you in the competition for any hard-to-win scholarship.

Furthermore, you may be participating in activities for which specific scholarships are awarded. Examples are the National Honor Society, the Distributive Education Club of America, and the Future Business Leaders of America.

> *Insider's advice:* If you are not active at all in this area, it is time to think about what extracurricular activities are of interest to you.

## Employment and Volunteer Work

It's almost always a good idea for a high school student to work. First of all, it will give you money to buy things you want. It also will teach you valuable work skills as you take on other student jobs, slowly but surely leading to a career after college graduation.

> *Insider's advice:* If one of your jobs happens to be in a field for which a scholarship is offered, so much the better. At this point you shouldn't concern yourself too much with this aspect of work. It is more important that you find a job you like and that pays reasonably well.
>
> The same advice holds for volunteer work. Try to do something that will help people in your school, church, or community. You should not be a volunteer because it looks good on a scholarship application.
>
> There are a number of scholarships that are connected to the occupations of your parents. It is unlikely that either of your parents will change their jobs to make it possible for you to compete for a scholarship. However, if the payoff is an educational benefit for which you automatically qualify, they may consider the possibility. (See pages 50–53 for an explanation of education benefits.)

Almost 8 percent of scholarship programs in Peterson's scholarship database were awarded on the basis of a student's or his or her parent's field of employment or employment by a particular company.

## Activities and Organizations Outside of School

Service organizations like Boy Scouts, Girl Scouts, and Future Farmers of America (student) and Lions, Elks, and Rotary (parents) give scholarships.

> **Insider's advice:** Parents should check with the organizations to which they belong to see if scholarships are offered.

In 1999–2000, slightly more than 22.5 percent of scholarship programs in Peterson's Non-Institutional Aid Database were awarded on the basis of a student's school activities, volunteer work outside of school, or the organizational affiliations of the student or parent.

## Religious Affiliation

Churches and synagogues are very active supporters of scholarships for their members. This includes the religions themselves as well as related organizations, like the Knights of Columbus (Roman Catholic) and the Memorial Foundation for Jewish Culture.

In 1999–2000, slightly more than 3.4 percent of scholarship programs in Peterson's Non-Institutional Aid Database were awarded on the basis of religious affiliation.

## Prior Military Service

Unless the student has enlisted in the Armed Forces between high school and college or is serving in the National Guard, this category is usually a parent attribute. Scholarships connected to prior military service are among the most widespread sources of college money.

The American Legion and the American Legion Auxiliary (the women's parallel organization) have been very active in establishing scholarships for veterans and their family members. There are national awards, but most are offered by state American Legion departments. A list of American Legion Department Web sites can be found at http://www.legion.org/dept.htm

> **Insider's advice:** If you are a veteran and a member of an American Legion post or a service-specific association, you should definitely check to see if there are scholarships available. If you are not currently a member but are thinking about joining, giving your child another possible scholarship option may help you make your decision.

Scholarships that are given in return for entering the military as an officer (service academies and ROTC) are discussed on pages 64–65.

# FURTHER COMMENTS ON SCHOLARSHIPS

### Be Sure to Place Scholarship Strategies in the Proper Context

Do not take a course, plan a career, join an organization, or start a job that you otherwise would not want to do only because it might increase your chance of winning a scholarship. The availability of a scholarship connected with a certain activity should be only one of the factors you weigh when you make academic and nonacademic choices.

### Grades Aren't Everything

The large majority of academic scholarships also look at the personal side of the student—strength of character, values, leadership, accomplishments, service to others, and participation in worthwhile activities. Build your credentials on the nonacademic side as you try to improve your grades.

### The Importance of Starting Early

If you are already halfway through your senior year in high school, the time you have to prepare yourself to win a scholarship has about run out. If, however, you are reading this book during your junior year, or even earlier, there may be steps you can take to improve your chance of winning a scholarship.

If you think about the academic credentials you will present to your college for admission, most of the weight will be given to what you have done through the end of your junior year. This includes grades, course requirements, standardized tests, extracurricular activities, and what you do outside of school. Making a strong "stretch run" in the fall of the senior year can add to your credentials, but there is a limit to how much it can improve the overall picture.

Competition for scholarships is much like the competition for admission at a selective college. The organization that sponsors the scholarship will evaluate your academic and nonacademic record in the same way that an admission committee does. The major difference is that you first have to meet the eligibility standard for the scholarship, for example plan to major in chemistry, be a Lutheran, be a member of the National Honor Society, or have a parent who is a military veteran.

## How Need and Merit Can Interact

At the beginning of this chapter, I gave you fairly simple explanations of a scholarship (a merit award) and a grant (a need award). These definitions still hold true, but it is necessary to further explain how these two types of gift aid are awarded.

Need grants sometimes have an element of merit, and merit scholarships sometimes have an element of need. The former (need modified by merit) is called **preferential packaging.** The latter has no formal name so we will simply label it as "scholarship amount varies with need."

### Preferential packaging

Preferential packaging is how a college recognizes a student's talents or accomplishments when making a need award. The amount of need is calculated in the normal way from the FAFSA (or PROFILE application). But when it comes to deciding how much grant, loan, and work-study (loan and job together are called **self-help**) will go into the total aid package, the most highly rated students get a larger amount of grant and less self-help compared to lower rated students.

———————————— ◇ ————————————

## EXAMPLE

Both Jim Jones and Sue Johnson have a need of $10,000. The college's admission office rates students in three categories—A, B, and C. Jim has an A rating and Sue a B rating. Under the college's preferential packaging policy, the following awards are given:

|  | Jim Jones | Sue Johnson |
|---|---|---|
| **Grant** | $ 8,000 | $ 4,000 |
| **Loan** | $ 1,000 | $ 4,000 |
| **Work-Study** | $ 1,000 | $ 2,000 |
| **TOTAL** | $10,000 | $10,000 |

Although both Jim and Sue have financial need of $10,000, due to the college's preferential packaging policy, Jim gets a much better award than Sue, with $4,000 more grant aid.

———————————— ◇ ————————————

### Scholarship amount varies with need

In a sense, this is the opposite of preferential packaging. These programs are fundamentally designed as scholarship competitions. Although the scholarship winners are chosen according to whom has the most outstanding record, the size of the award is governed by need.

The scholarship selection committee usually sets up a sliding scale where the most highly rated students with the most need get the largest awards, lower rated with less need the next highest amount, and on down until the winners who don't demonstrate need receive honorary awards.

**The National Merit Scholarship** competition is organized this way. A non-needy winner receives an honorary award of

$2,000 per year for four years. A needy winner can receive as much as $8,000. A description of the National Merit Scholarship program can be found at http://www.nationalmerit.org.

What does this intermingling of the concepts of need and merit mean for you?

It means that even if you are applying to a college with an extensive need aid program, your admission credentials (as well as your level of need) are likely to effect how much grant you receive.

## SUMMARY OF KEY POINTS

- Scholarships and education benefits are the best forms of aid. They don't require a needs test and they don't have to be repaid.

- Before you enter the aid process, you should take a personal inventory and see how your characteristics and attributes fit with scholarship requirements.

- You should try a free Internet scholarship search, the earlier the better. If, for example, you begin in your junior year in high school, you will have time to devise a scholarship strategy that will increase your chances of winning an award. Also, by your junior year, find out what the requirements are for your state's academic scholarship and shoot for the GPA that will enable you to win an award.

- In addition to the Internet, your high school guidance office and public library are good sources of scholarship information.

- When you first develop your college list and receive admission material, read the financial aid section to see how to apply for college scholarships.

# REDUCING THE TOLL II: HOW TO FIND GRANTS AND OTHER NEED AID

- How to determine if you might qualify for need aid
- Estimate your EFC
- Estimate college costs
- Estimate need
- Learn about college aid policies
- The aid applications
- Awarding financial aid
- Summary of key points

It is now time to learn more about the largest—by far—form of aid: need-based grants, loans, and work-study. You first have to decide whether or not it is worthwhile to apply for aid. If the answer is yes, you will have to determine which applications are required and when they are due.

## HOW TO DETERMINE IF YOU MIGHT QUALIFY FOR NEED AID

Unless you are sure you will not demonstrate need at the most expensive college on your list, you should go through the relatively painless process of finding out if you might qualify.

To make this determination, you start with two ingredients:

- the Expected Family Contribution (EFC)
- the cost of the college.

If the EFC is less than the cost of attendance, you qualify for need aid. If your EFC is more than the cost, you are "no-need." If you are no-need, you still qualify for the scholarships described in Chapter 4, Reducing the Toll I: How to Find Scholarships. Also see the section "If You Are Not Receiving Aid" on page 104 in Chapter 6.

## ESTIMATE YOUR EFC

The easiest way to do this is to use an EFC estimator on the Internet. Before you go to the EFC estimator, gather together:

- Parents' taxable and nontaxable income for 1999, actual or estimated.

*Note:* Even if your child will not attend college until after the 2000–2001 academic year, this is the year for which the estimator is programmed if you enter data between September 1999 and August 2000.

- Current parental assets, not counting home value.

*Note:* You will need to determine your home equity (market value less mortgage) if you decide to use PROFILE's Institutional Methodology. See pages 86–89 for more information about PROFILE.

- Student's taxable and nontaxable income

- Student assets

- Number of family members and number of children in college for the 2000–2001 academic year. (If you are using the 2000–2001 estimator to get a rough EFC for a later year, use the number of family members and children in college for the year your child will attend.)

Enter the information in the early estimator and make a note of your EFC.

**Use one of the following EFC Estimators:**

- **http://www.collegequest.com/** Go to "Financial Aid," click on "Applying for and Receiving Financial Aid," click on "Entering the Need-Based System," and click on "EFC Estimator."

- **http://www.finaid.org/** Go to "Calculators," click on "Needs Analysis," and click on "Financial Aid Estimation."

- **http://www.collegeboard.org/** Go to "Students and Parents," under "Services," click on "Financial Aid Calculators," and click on "Expected Family Contribution."

- **http://www.salliemae.com/** Go to "Calculators" and click on "Expected Family Contribution Calculator."

The estimators will give you the option of choosing either the FAFSA's Federal Methodology (FM) or PROFILE's Institutional Methodology (IM) need formula. For an early estimate of your EFC, the FM result is satisfactory. Later on, if you include a PROFILE college on your list, you can also try the IM calculation to see if there is much of a difference.

## ESTIMATE COLLEGE COSTS

Go to http://www.collegequest.com. Click on "Pick," and then click on "Alphabetical Look-up." When you enter a college and click on that college, you will go to a page that shows the costs.

It is likely that only tuition, room, and board charges will be shown. If so, add $2,000 for books and personal expense and a travel allowance. If you plan to commute rather than live on campus, use $2,900 rather than the college's room and board.

Since the costs listed are probably for the 1998–99 or 1999–2000 academic year, multiply the total budget you have come up with by 1.05 if 1999–2000 costs are shown or by 1.10 if 1998–99 costs are listed.

## ESTIMATE NEED

Compare the EFC with the cost of each college and see if there is a chance you will qualify for need aid. If you are clearly eligible or if it is a close call, plan to apply for aid. Even if this early estimate shows you to be no-need, there may be other reasons why you should fill out a FAFSA. For example, you might have special circumstances that would permit a campus financial aid administrator to lower your EFC based on professional judgement.

**If you decide to apply for aid,** read the rest of this chapter about the need aid process.

**If you decide not to apply,** concentrate on non-need aid—education benefits and scholarships—found in Chapter 4, Reducing the Toll I: How to Find Scholarships. Also see the section "If You Are Not Receiving Financial Aid" on page 104 in Chapter 6.

## LEARN ABOUT COLLEGE AID POLICIES

**Read the financial aid section of the college admission material carefully.**

Make a list of what forms are required along with their deadlines. Read the description of each college's policies and practices so you have a good understanding of the aid program.

**Get answers to these questions:**

1. Are your chances of being admitted any different if you apply for aid? (In other words, is the college "need blind"?)

2. Does the college meet 100 percent of need?

3. If the college doesn't meet 100 percent of need, how much of a gap does it leave?

4. Does the college have its own grant (need-based) funds, or does it only administer federal, state, and private funds?

5. Does the college have its own scholarship (merit-based) funds? If yes, what programs does it have, and what are the eligibility standards?

6. Does the college have any scholarships that require an application other than FAFSA or PROFILE?

7. Does the college consider special family circumstances, or is it strict about following the federal need formula?

If these questions, or others that you might have, are not answered in the college's material, call or visit the aid office.

*Insider's Advice:* If you think you will qualify for need aid (or possibly win a scholarship), do not eliminate a college you would like to attend because of its sticker price. It is unlikely that you will pay the full cost, but you will not know your actual cost until a financial aid decision has been made. On many occasions I have seen a higher-cost college require a smaller family contribution than a lower-cost college. The time to weigh costs in your decision about which college to attend is when you know your actual out-of-pocket expense at each college where you have been admitted.

# THE AID APPLICATIONS

There are as many as five possibilities, although most applicants will only have to fill out the FAFSA.

1. FAFSA
2. PROFILE
3. Your state aid application
4. A college aid application
5. Applications for private awards

## The FAFSA

This is the application for federal Title IV programs, most state need-based aid, and a good portion of college need-based aid.

> **Insider's Advice:** *When in doubt, fill it out.*
>
> Although it may look like a tax return, the FAFSA works in the opposite direction. It is not used to figure how much you have to pay, but how much you will receive. *And you aren't going to get need aid without it.*

There are probably thousands of families that would qualify for aid (if not a grant, at least a subsidized student loan) if they could bring themselves to complete the FAFSA.

The most common reason given for not filing the FAFSA is that it is too complicated. Although the FAFSA may look intimidating (the application and the instructions are about eight pages), once you get the proper information together, it's not difficult to fill out.

One of the advantages of using an early EFC estimator is to give you a practice run with the process. Once you have taken the time to get your information together, read the estimator instructions, and respond to the questions, you will be prepared to deal with the actual FAFSA.

The other comment I hear from families that are reluctant to fill out the FAFSA is the "big brother" concern—"I don't want to send my financial information to the federal government because I don't know what they are going to do with it." The FAFSA is a confidential document that is used to award aid. There is a section on the FAFSA that explains the organizations with whom the Department of Education is allowed to share information. The Privacy Act prohibits any other use of your data.

It is important for you to overcome any reluctance you might have to complete the FAFSA since *it is the only way you can claim your share of the $52 billion in need aid available each year.*

## How to get it

The paper form is available in your high school, public library, or college financial aid office.

There is an Internet version, FAFSA on the Web, that you can complete and send the FAFSA electronically at http://www.fafsa.ed.gov.

There is a further option called FAFSA Express that requires you to download software and complete the form on your own computer. This version is available at http://www.ed.gov/offices/ope/express.html.

> *Insider's Advice:* If you are on line, you might as well go ahead and use FAFSA on the Web and avoid the extra work of downloading software.

Currently, both electronic versions require a signature page sent by regular mail. However, the Department of Education is working on a system that will allow families to certify their FAFSAs over the Internet.

The following are Department of Education Web sites that give financial aid information:

- Master Department of Education site: http://www.ed.gov/studentaid

- FAFSA Help: http://www.ed.gov/prog_info/sfa/fafsa

- *The Student Guide* on the Web: http://www.ed.gov/prog_info/sfa/studentguide

- *Funding Your Education:* http://www.ed.gov/prog_info/sfa/fye

## How to fill it out

Before you start to complete the FAFSA (we are assuming your aid application is for the 2000–2001 academic year), collect the information you will need:

- Actual or draft copies of the parent and student 1999 tax returns you plan to send to the IRS. Nearly all college financial aid deadlines fall after February 1, so you should have your W-2 forms and other reports of earnings

- A list of parent and student 1999 nontaxable income. FAFSA worksheets A and B show the various categories

- An accounting of parent and student assets as of the date you fill out the FAFSA. Do this in four categories:

  1. Cash, savings, and checking
  2. Net worth of investments
  3. Net worth of business
  4. Net worth of farm

The instructions explain which assets to report. Do not include the value of life insurance, retirement plans, prepaid tuition programs, or the equity in your home.

> ***Self-supporting students:*** If you are an independent student, parental information is not required. See Chapter 8, Side Roads: Nontraditional Students, for the definition of an independent student.

You are now ready to complete the FAFSA. You should read the general instructions before you start and refer to the explanations for individual questions if you are not clear about what information is required.

If you have special circumstances, notify the financial aid office at your colleges. Do not send any additional material with your FAFSA; it will be thrown away.

You will need the federal school code for each of your colleges. Your high school guidance office should have a copy of the code book. If not, the codes are listed on the Internet at http://www.ed.gov/offices/OSFAP.

## Divorced/separated parents

If your parents are divorced or separated, follow the instructions. Only the custodial parent is required to complete the FAFSA, unless that person has remarried. In that case, both the custodial parent and the stepparent submit their information (the same rules hold for PROFILE).

Expecting the stepparent to assume the same level of responsibility to pay for college as would be expected of the natural parent can cause a problem. Unfortunately, federal rules clearly spell out that the custodial natural parent and the stepparent are the "family unit" for awarding aid. Financial aid administrators are not permitted to waive the stepparent requirement.

Some colleges that use PROFILE (see pages 86–89) may send you a "Noncustodial Parent's Statement" for your other parent to complete. This form is used when the custodial parent has not remarried. As mentioned above, if the custodial parent has remarried, the stepparent's information is used rather than the natural parent's.

On occasion, the noncustodial parent has completely disassociated himself or herself from the student applicant. In this case, you should ask the PROFILE college to waive the "Noncustodial Parent's Statement" requirement. If you haven't been in contact with your other parent for a period of time (five years is often used), there is a good chance that you will receive a waiver.

### FAFSA Strategies—How to Maximize Your Aid Eligibility

From what I've observed, it seems as though no book on financial aid is complete without a section on tips for filling out the FAFSA. My general view is there are not very many strategies that are practical and also will result in you receiving more aid than you otherwise would have.

On the issue of practicability, I have read aid books that tell you to lower your income by taking capital gains during the tenth grade so your income for the next year (the year used to make the freshman year award) is less than it would have been. For most of you, even if you report capital gains, your child's tenth grade year has probably already passed.

Furthermore, even if you can figure out a way to report lower income or assets, you probably won't receive any more grant aid. Let me give you an example.

Suppose you transfer $5,000 of your assets to a nonreportable category. Your EFC will decrease by about $300, and you will have $300 more of need. The college's most likely action is to let you borrow an extra $300 or, if you already have the maximum loan, to increase your "gap" by $300 (in other words, not give you any more aid).

The inability of most families to move their income around and the uncertainty that more need will mean more grant dollars means that there are not very many FAFSA strategies that are effective. Furthermore, keep in mind that whatever you do, you have to certify that your FAFSA information is true and correct. Considering all of this, there are still some possible strategies.

### Six Tips for Lowering Your EFC

1. Keep parental savings in the parents' name, not the child's. You will lose more under the need formula than you gain from a reduction in income taxes.

2. If grandparents want to help pay for college, have them keep the money in their name and use it to help pay the college bill rather than give the funds to your child ahead of time.

3. If you are going to pay off your consumer debt from your savings around the time your child applies for aid, do it before you complete the FAFSA. The same goes for using savings to make a large purchase, like a car.

4. If you have the opportunity to classify income as either yours (the parents') or the child's, report all income over $2,200 as parental income.

5. When it is time to pay the college bill, spend student assets before parental assets.

6. Maximize contributions to your retirement fund, since it is a nonreportable asset.

---

***This one doesn't work anymore.*** The most common FAFSA strategy you will find in aid books is to have one or both parents enroll in college. (The more family members you have in college, the less the EFC for any one.) The Department of Education has caught on to this trick and changed the need formula to count only dependent children in college.

---

If you would like to go beyond my six tips and look into this subject in greater detail, I recommend the "Maximizing Your Aid Eligibility" section under "Financial Aid Applications" at http://www.finaid.org.

**What to do if you have a problem**

First, refer to the detailed instructions included with the paper copy or on the Internet. If you are still struggling with the form, check with your high school guidance counselor to see what help is available. If the counselor cannot be of assistance, phone the financial aid office at a local college or a college you are applying to. Another option is to contact the Department of Education directly. The Department of Education Help Line phone number is 800-433-3243 (toll-free). All these resources are free. You should not have to pay someone to help you complete the FAFSA.

**How to submit the FAFSA**

Do not file the FAFSA before January 1 of the year you begin college. This means after January 1, 2000, for the 2000–2001 academic year, after January 1, 2001, for the 2001–2002 academic year, and so forth. Mail the paper copy or submit the Internet version. If you use FAFSA on the Web, don't forget to mail a separate signature page

In about three to four weeks, you will receive a Student Aid Report (SAR) that will summarize the information you entered on the FAFSA and list the colleges where you want your information sent. The SAR will also show your EFC in the upper right hand corner.

Questions about the processing status of your FAFSA should be directed to 319-337-5665.

> **Insider's Advice**: If any of your deadlines fall before you have completed you tax return, use your best estimate of income. Do not delay filing the FAFSA; you can send corrected figures later.

---◇---

## STAY ON TOP OF THE AID PROCESS

### Pay attention to deadlines.

Make sure you meet the earliest deadline set by a college or other scholarship program. Some financial programs will not consider late applications. Others award money on a first come, first served basis. The later you are, the less chance you have of receiving aid.

### Keep copies of everything you submit, and make a note of when they were mailed.

Double check that you haven't missed anything. It may be that your state, one of your colleges, or a private organization has a scholarship that requires a separate application.

---◇---

## PROFILE

If a college on your list also asks for PROFILE, you'll have to submit it in addition to the FAFSA.

This aid application form comes from the College Scholarship Service, a division of the College Board. PROFILE is used by colleges that have their own scholarship funds and want to do a more careful calculation of need than is possible with the FAFSA. While the FAFSA is free, there is a charge for PROFILE. For 1999–2000, the price of PROFILE was $20 for the first college and $15 for each additional college.

## Differences between PROFILE and the FAFSA

Why should you have to fill out two financial aid applications? The simple reason is that about 300 colleges require PROFILE. Although PROFILE entails extra work and added expense, *it opens the door to more than $2 billion in college gift aid.*

If you qualify for aid, the cost of completing the PROFILE application is usually worth it because you may receive a college grant in addition to federal and state assistance.

PROFILE is similar to the FAFSA. The main difference is that PROFILE collects more information about a family's financial situation. It also provides white space for families to explain special circumstances and contains supplemental questions that help colleges assign restricted scholarships and grants.

In contrast to the FAFSA, PROFILE's Institutional Methodology (IM) need formula includes the value of the family home as a countable asset and expects a minimum student contribution. These two factors can lead to a higher IM EFC than Federal Methodology (FM).

On the other hand, IM includes a number of allowances (like medical, private secondary school tuition, and college savings) that can lower the IM EFC compared to FM. Also, a recent change in the IM reduces the contribution rate on student assets from 35 percent (this is still the FM rate) to 25 percent.

Another advantage of PROFILE is that the financial aid administrators at PROFILE colleges have more information about a family's special circumstances and therefore are more likely to exercise professional judgement.

### How to get it

There are two ways to receive paper copies of PROFILE.

- **by phone:** call 800-778-6888 (toll-free).

- **on the Internet:** go to http://www.collegeboard.org. Click on "CSS/Financial Aid PROFILE." Click on "Register for a paper PROFILE Application." You also can register for and complete PROFILE on line. Click on "CSS/Financial Aid PROFILE." Click on "Complete PROFILE Online" and follow the instructions. You will need a credit card to pay the fee.

### How to fill it out

Since PROFILE is used for early decision admission programs, it can be completed as early as October 15 of the year prior to the year of attendance (October 15, 1999, for the 2000–2001 academic year).

For regular admission decision programs, most PROFILE colleges require the form by March 1.

Because of the earlier PROFILE deadlines, it is likely you will complete PROFILE before you file your tax return. Make your best estimate of 1999 income. The college you decide to attend usually will ask you to verify the income with a copy of your tax return.

Collect the information you need before you start. Refer to the list in the previous section for the FAFSA. The data that is required is essentially the same, with the exception that you will have to report your prior year income as well as your home equity (market value minus mortgage) on PROFILE.

You are now ready to complete PROFILE. First read the general instructions. If you don't understand a question, refer to the individual explanations.

### What to do if you have a problem

Depending on the question, your high school guidance office is usually the first place to go. If your question is complicated or involves confidential information, check with a financial aid administrator at one of the PROFILE colleges on your list. You also can contact the PROFILE help line at 305-829-9793 with your questions.

**How to submit it**

Mail the paper copy with the appropriate fee, or use your credit card to pay for the online version.

In about three weeks, you will be sent an acknowledgment, which will list the colleges where your information will be sent. If there are changes in your family's financial circumstances after you have completed the PROFILE, notify your colleges directly.

## State Grant Applications

Some states run their grant programs entirely from the FAFSA, while others ask for a separate application. Your high school guidance office should have material about your state grant program that explains the application procedure. If this information is not available in your high school, contact the state agency directly. A list of state higher education agencies and their Web sites appears in Appendix A.

## College Applications

For the purpose of awarding grants, most colleges rely on the FAFSA, while a few hundred also require PROFILE. In addition to the two national aid applications, some colleges have their own forms that are returned directly to the campus financial aid office. These applications are included with the admission material and are usually quite easy to fill out.

## Private Scholarship and Grant Applications

As described in Chapter 4, Reducing the Toll I: How to Find Scholarships, a separate application is almost always necessary for a private scholarship. If the gift aid (either a scholarship or grant) has a need component, the sponsor will ask for family financial information on the form.

## What Happens to the FAFSA and PROFILE?

Either by mail or on the Internet, your application goes to a processing center. A need formula is applied to your financial data to get an EFC. A list of the data you entered as well as the EFC goes to you, your colleges, and other authorized aid programs.

> ***Important point:*** The financial aid administrator is not required to accept the central processor's calculation of the EFC. The aid system allows for the exercise of professional judgement at the campus level. This discretion, however, is not unlimited, since there are both federal and institutional guidelines that have to be followed. Nevertheless, you should know that the central processor does not ultimately determine your EFC; the financial aid administrator on campus does.

# AWARDING FINANCIAL AID

Once the aid administrator has come up with your EFC, it is subtracted from your cost of attendance to determine if you have need. If you do, the college will send you an award letter that contains an aid package.

The aid package will consist of some combination of:

- gift aid (scholarship, educational benefit, or grant)
- student subsidized loan
- work-study job.

Once you have been admitted and have an award decision, it is time to go to the next chapter, Choosing a Destination: The Role of Aid in Selecting a College.

If you are judged no-need and nevertheless feel you require financial assistance, see "If You Are Not Receiving Aid" on page 104 in Chapter 6.

# SUMMARY OF KEY POINTS

Estimate your EFC, compare it to college costs, and decide if it's worthwhile to apply for aid. If you do:

- Read the college financial aid material, and follow the application instructions.

- Complete the FAFSA (and PROFILE if required) by the earliest deadline specified by your college, state, or other organization.

- Complete any other aid application.

- Keep a copy of the forms and a calendar of what you've done.

- Depending on the topic, direct questions to your guidance counselor, the FAFSA or PROFILE customer line, or a financial aid office.

- If your family has special financial circumstances, visit or write the aid office.

# CHAPTER 6

# CHOOSING A DESTINATION: THE ROLE OF AID IN SELECTING A COLLEGE

- Cost of attendance
- Determine how much "good" aid you have
- Calculate your family financial responsibility
- If you have a gap
- Dealing with the financial aid office
- If you are not receiving aid
- Summary of key points

You have now been accepted by one or more colleges. If you were an aid applicant, you have a decision—either an award or a letter saying that you are ineligible. The other possibility is that you didn't apply for aid, but now, as you look at the cost, you and your parents are worried about where the money is going to come from. To read about available assistance in these latter two situations (no-need and non-aid), go to pages 104–106.

But for now, let's turn our attention to aided students. It is important that you read the award letter carefully and the material that comes with it. If there is something you don't understand, call or visit the financial aid office. Here are some things you should know.

## COST OF ATTENDANCE (COA)

The COA should be indicated in the award letter (or on an information sheet) so you are able to come up with your total budget. If you cannot determine your cost of attendance, contact the financial aid office for assistance.

Your COA is based primarily on two factors:

- your academic program
- your living (and eating) arrangements.

A tuition and fee charge will be determined from your enrollment status (full- or part-time), and course of study (credit hours, lab courses, and other charges).

If you will live on campus, your COA will include room and board, usually starting with a standard amount and adjusted when you select a specific dormitory and meal plan. If you live off-campus, your allowance for room and board will probably will be based on the on-campus rate.

If you are going to travel back and forth from home rather than live at the college, the COA will be built on a commuting budget. The standard practice is to replace the room and board charge with a $2,000 commuting allowance and use $900 for travel costs, although the actual amounts will be set by your college.

Many colleges publish a figure called the comprehensive fee, which includes tuition, fees, room, and board. Sometimes the comprehensive fee is referred to as "billable costs."

But billable costs are not the only expenses that make up the COA. The other items that you will have to pay for are books, personal expenses (laundry, furnishings, supplies, telephone, clothes, etc.), and travel. If the college has not given you a figure for your books and personal expenses, you will need to come up with an estimate. I suggest you check with the financial aid administrator for guidance.

*Insider's Advice:* Take the time to estimate a COA for each of your colleges. It is impossible to figure out how much you have to pay unless you have a good idea of your yearly COA.

# DETERMINE HOW MUCH "GOOD" AID YOU HAVE

All financial aid is not created equal.

Good aid is:

- all gift aid (clearly the most desirable)
- a subsidized student loan
- work-study

Student loans and work-study are known as self-help, since they require an obligation on the part of the student. Need should only be met with one of these three forms of assistance.

Less desirable aid is:

- unsubsidized student loan
- non–work-study job
- parental loan.

These types of aid should not be used to meet need, although some colleges will include one or more of them in your aid package.

As you evaluate your awards and compare them among colleges, you should consider unsubsidized student loans, non–work-study student employment, and parental loans as part of the family financial responsibility, not as need aid.

> *Insider's Advice:* Read your award letter carefully so you can add up your good aid.

## Gift Aid

Know if there are any conditions attached to the scholarship or grant you have been awarded, including the college's policy for renewing your aid.

If you have an outside scholarship, check to see if it has been included in your aid package. Find out what the college's policy is when there is an outside scholarship in your award. This is particularly important if you have not yet won an award but expect to.

## Subsidized Student Loan

This is a loan that is interest free while you are in college. If your loan is subsidized, the federal government pays the yearly interest to the lender during your enrollment period. The award letter should make it clear whether your loan is subsidized. If it is not clear, ask.

The three large subsidized federal student loan programs are the **Direct, Stafford,** and **Perkins**.

Of these three, Perkins is the best loan because it has the lowest (5 percent) interest rate. Direct and Stafford loans have the same terms, with a current interest rate of about 7 percent.

It is important that you know from reading your award letter whether or not your Stafford or Direct loan is subsidized, since there are both subsidized and unsubsidized versions. (All Perkins loans are subsidized.)

If the loan is unsubsidized, you pay the interest each year. The money you save if you have a subsidized loan rather than an unsubsidized loan can be substantial. If you borrow the maximum undergraduate unsubsidized Stafford or Direct loan, you will pay an extra $2,600 in interest charges. During your repayment period, for ten years after you graduate, you pay the same interest rate on either the subsidized or unsubsidized loan.

## Work-study

This is a need-based job where you are assigned a position on campus and given enough hours to meet your earning expectation. Work-study is good aid in contrast to a job where you have to search out an employer (perhaps off-campus) and arrange your own work schedule. There is also no assurance you will be able to work the necessary hours.

# A Hierarchy of Aid

As you evaluate the components of your award letter, here is an approximate pecking order of aid, from most desirable to least desirable.

1. **Scholarship with added benefits,** like an extra stipend to do summer study.

2. **Scholarship with minimum requirements for renewal,** like satisfactory progress or a B average.

3. **Need-based grant;** amount depends on a reevaluation of need each year.

4. **Scholarship with obligations,** e.g., ROTC, athletic grant-in-aid, or a college scholarship, that requires a high GPA or restricts your major or career choice.

5. **A work-study job** with placement by the aid office, good pay, and interesting work—perhaps career or academic related.

6. **Subsidized student loan with cancellation of repayment** for work in the career that you plan to pursue.

7. **Subsidized student loan,** especially the lower–interest rate Perkins.

8. **Academic year employment, where you have to find your own job** and you are not assured of the work hours you need.

9. **An unsubsidized Stafford/Direct loan,** where the interest is due yearly, or an alternative student loan. (*Note:* An alternative student loan is defined as a nonfederal education loan. Some colleges offer their own alternative loans. More common are the education loan programs of lenders such as Sallie Mae, Citicorp, or USA Group.)

10. **A parental loan.** This is another form of aid that is usually less desirable than any of the above. However, under certain conditions, a parental loan (perhaps a home equity line of credit) might have more favorable terms than the unsubsidized Stafford/Direct or alternative loan. Before taking out a parental loan, compare the terms to student loan options.

# CALCULATE YOUR FAMILY FINANCIAL RESPONSIBILITY

By now, you should have the COA for each of your colleges and know what good aid you have received. Use a worksheet like the one below to list your colleges, their costs, and good aid. Subtract the aid from the COA. The result is the amount of your family financial responsibility (FFR). The FFR is the sum of the resources you need (after aid) to pay the cost of a year of college.

When you calculate the FFR, you will be able to see for the first time how much your family actually has to pay for college.

You also can compare your bottom line obligation for each of your colleges. By asking you to use only good aid to reduce the COA, I have tried to match "apples with apples" by assuming any less desirable aid you receive is part of the FFR.

## Award Comparison Worksheet

|  | College 1 | College 2 | College 3 | College 4 |
|---|---|---|---|---|
| **COA:** | | | | |
| Tuition | | | | |
| Room and Board | | | | |
| Books | | | | |
| Personal | | | | |
| Travel | | | | |
| TOTAL | | | | |
| **Good Aid:** | | | | |
| Gift Aid (scholarships or grants) | | | | |
| Subsidized student loan | | | | |
| Work-study | | | | |
| TOTAL | | | | |

Subtract good aid from the COA to get your FFR.

| FFR | | | | |
|---|---|---|---|---|

**Looking More Closely at the FFR**

The first reason for calculating the FFR is to help you figure out where you are going to get the money to pay for college. The second is to allow you to compare different financial aid awards. The Family Financial Responsibility worksheet will make these tasks easier for you.

Your next step is to figure out your total available resources—how much money you can put together to pay for college. Compare your total available resources from your FFR (on the Award Comparison Worksheet).

---

**Family Financial Responsibility Worksheet**

|  | College 1 | College 2 | College 3 | College 4 |
|---|---|---|---|---|
| How much can you afford from parents' income and assets? | _____ | _____ | _____ | _____ |
| How much can you afford from student's assets? | _____ | _____ | _____ | _____ |
| **TOTAL available resources** | _____ | _____ | _____ | _____ |

Compare your total available resources with your FFR (on the Award Comparison Worksheet).

---

If your total available resources equal the FFR, the college's financial aid award has worked for you—you are able to pay what is needed and there is no gap. If this occurs at your first choice college, there is no financial barrier to accepting the admission offer. If the FFR is more than your available resources, you have a gap, or a shortfall, in what is needed to cover the cost.

> ***Note:*** Before you seek out other forms of assistance, you should review your COA to see if reductions can be made. Lowering your expenses will reduce the gap the same way as adding aid. You should check with the financial aid administrator for advice if this is an option you would like to pursue.

If you have a gap

While the no-gap situation may be true for some of your colleges, you may have a gap at others. If you want to continue to consider colleges where you have a gap, it is necessary to look for additional resources.

**Possible additional resources**

- **More good financial aid**. You could make an appeal to the financial aid office and ask for additional assistance—gift aid, subsidized loan, or work-study.

- **Outside scholarships**. Perhaps you are in the running for a scholarship or you know of awards that you can apply for. Before you go too far with this option, ask the financial aid administrator how the receipt of an outside scholarship will effect your aid package.

- **Additional student loan or work.** Once you've exhausted the possibility of receiving more subsidized loan or work-study, you can ask about unsubsidized loans (either Stafford/Direct or an alternative loan) and access to jobs on and off campus.

- **Parental loan**. Because it is not always possible to get enough total student aid to cover the FFR, parental loans have become a common means of paying for college. The federal government sponsors the Parent Loans for Undergraduate Students (PLUS) program, and most of the companies that provide alternative student loans offer parental loans as well. The college financial aid administrator can give you information about PLUS and alternative loans.

*Insider's Advice:* If you are interested in attending a college where you have a gap, you will need to come up with a plan to fill the shortfall with additional aid from one or more of the above sources or reduce your COA.

# DEALING WITH THE FINANCIAL AID OFFICE

The aid office can be a busy place, especially right after award letters go out. But if you have questions, do not hesitate to contact them. It is the role of the aid office to make it financially possible for admitted students to attend their college.

If the aid office has not sent you a complete award letter that gives aid, costs, and the family contribution, your first contact with an aid administrator should be to get the information you need to be able to enter the numbers in the Award Comparison Worksheet.

**Do's and don'ts in dealing with the financial aid office**

- Don't contact the financial aid office until you have carefully read the award letter and other material that comes with it.

- Do contact the aid office if you have a question that is not covered in the material.

- Do work out a financial plan (the worksheets in this chapter simplify the process) to see whether you can afford to attend the colleges that have admitted you.

- Do contact the aid office if you can't put together the resources that will enable you to attend.

- Don't contact the aid office without a specific reason. "My neighbor said I should make sure I call the financial aid office" or "I read in a magazine that financial aid is actually a negotiating process" are not specific reasons.

- Do contact the aid office if there has been a change in your family financial circumstances since you filed your aid application.

- Do meet the deadlines for accepting your financial aid and returning time-sensitive material.

> **Insider's Advice:** For routine matters, a phone call is the easiest means of contact. Letters, e-mail, and faxes are also good forms of communication, especially when details have to be spelled out. For serious problems, a personal visit is recommended, but always make an appointment first. Be sure to bring information to support the point you want to make.

### Looking for more aid

If the Family Financial Responsibility Worksheet showed a gap, more than likely you will need the help of an aid administrator.

First of all, have him or her confirm the assumptions you have made about your cost of attendance, aid package, family financial responsibility, and gap.

Once there is agreement on the amount of the shortfall that has to be covered, ask for advice on where to find additional sources of aid (or ways to reduce the cost of attendance) that were described on page 100.

The purpose of meeting with an aid administrator is for you to work out a plan where you can get the additional resources you need to attend that college. If this is not possible, you may have to turn to another college on your list.

> **Insider's Advice:** You should have a financial problem-solving discussion with an aid administrator at your first-choice college before you decide you cannot attend for financial aid reasons.

### Negotiation

I do not classify the type of aid discussion mentioned above as a negotiating tactic. Financial aid administrators have these conversations all the time, and a good portion of their jobs is devoted to helping families work out a successful financial plan.

The idea of negotiation as a technique that will get your child more aid has been blown out of proportion by the media. Financial aid administrators don't like to use the term "negotiate." They refer to a request by a family to change an award as an **appeal.**

## Appeals

There are two types of appeals:

- financial

- competitive.

## Financial

This is the situation where a family can't afford its contribution and needs additional help.

A financial appeal is not considered negotiation. The success of your appeal will depend mainly on a reevaluation of your family's ability to pay for college.

How much aid is given and the type of aid (it can range anywhere from more scholarship or grant to an unsubsidized loan) depends on the strength of the appeal, the amount of money still available, and how highly you are rated by the admission office.

## Competitive

This refers to a request for more aid because another college has a better award. The response to a family that asks the aid office to match (or exceed) another college's offer will vary a great deal among different institutions.

The large majority of colleges will already have given you their best offer and don't have the money to do more. There are, however, a hundred colleges or so (mainly private colleges with their own scholarship funds) that will consider a competitive appeal. In fact, some of these will even encourage you to get in touch with them if another college makes a better offer.

If you feel that your child is one of the college's highly rated admits, it doesn't hurt to ask for more money. But do it politely and don't be surprised if the college doesn't engage in the practice.

# IF YOU ARE NOT RECEIVING AID

It is not only financial aid recipients who are concerned about how to pay for college. You may find yourself without aid and be worried about where the money is going to come from. Before you consider the option of choosing a less expensive college that is not your number-one choice, you should carefully look into all of the possible resources mentioned below.

## No-Need

"No-need" is a term to refer to a family that applied for aid but was judged to have adequate resources to pay for college. You probably applied for aid because you felt you did not have enough money to pay the bill. If you have been told that you don't qualify, you are in nearly the same situation as an aided family with a gap.

> ***Insider's Advice***: Before you rule out any chance of need aid, you should ask yourself if there are any special circumstances that have not been brought to the attention of the financial aid office. If your answer to this question is yes, I recommend that you visit the financial aid office and talk with a counselor. You still can ask for help even though you are not on aid. You should bring information that supports your case and have an idea of how much assistance you need to close your gap. You should always exhaust the possibility of need aid before you turn to other forms of assistance.

If you are unsuccessful in an appeal for need-based aid, you will be limited to the following:

- Lowering your cost of attendance

- Finding a merit scholarship

- Locating other student resources—non–work-study student employment, unsubsidized Stafford or Direct loans, or alternative student loans

- Applying for a parental loan, either PLUS or an alternative program

## Non-aid

There are always some families that don't apply for aid but later encounter difficulties when they see the size of the tuition bill. There can be various reasons why you might find yourself in this position.

- You didn't want to deal with the financial aid process, so you didn't file the FAFSA.

- Your family financial circumstances have worsened in recent months.

- Your child was accepted by a college that is more expensive than you had anticipated.

If one of these descriptions fits you, visit the financial aid office and see if you might still qualify for aid. You can always fill out a FAFSA (up until May of your freshman year) and find out if you are eligible for a Pell grant, state grant, or subsidized student loan. Remaining aid funds are controlled by the college, and they may already have been assigned to other students. Nevertheless, it doesn't hurt to ask what happens if you should qualify for aid after the college's deadline has passed.

If you decided to submit a FAFSA and did not demonstrate need, or if know you will not qualify, you should try to reduce your COA and look into the non-need resources:

- merit scholarships

- student employment other than work-study

- unsubsidized Stafford or Direct loans

- alternative student loans

- PLUS parental loan

- alternative parental loans.

## SUMMARY OF KEY POINTS

- You need a good estimate of your COA before you can determine how much you will have to pay.

- Some colleges will mix good aid with less desirable aid in the same package. You should know the difference.

- After good aid is subtracted from the COA, the remainder is your family financial responsibility.

- To attend the college of your choice, you must come up with sufficient resources to meet your family financial responsibility.

- Using the proper approach in dealing with the financial aid office will increase your chances of receiving more aid.

- Although it may work on occasion, don't expect to negotiate your way to a better award.

- Even if you are not on aid, there is assistance available.

# CHAPTER 7

# Paying the Toll: You've Selected a College, It's Time to Pay the Bill

- An aid award checklist
- Your student loan
- Alternative aid sources
- Payment plans
- Tuition tax credits
- Summary of key points

You have now applied to college, been admitted, decided which college to attend, and have some idea of how the bill will be paid. Congratulations!

From this point on, you will take care of money matters directly with your college. The two most important offices are:

- the financial aid office (even if you are not on aid, that is still the first place to go if you have a financial problem)

- the student accounts office, sometimes called the bursar.

However, before I leave you on your own to deal with aid and bill payment issues, I would like to give you a few tips to make sure you are on the right track.

## AN AID AWARD CHECKLIST

✔ Find your award letter and the material that came with it. Reread the information to make sure you understand the components and your rights and responsibilities.

- Make your own list of what you need to do to finalize the award. Usually, there are a number of forms to complete and return to the aid office. Some of the most common are the award acceptance, copies of student and parent tax returns, selection of a Stafford lender, and report of outside scholarships.

- If your scholarship or grant has conditions attached to it, you should know what they are and plan to meet the standards. The most common requirement is to maintain a certain grade point average.

- If you have an outside scholarship, ask the sponsor to send the check to the college as soon as possible. You want to have the money available when the first bill is due.

- If there has been an adverse change in your family's financial circumstances since you completed the FAFSA, you should let the aid office know. By midsummer, you should try to firm up your award so the college bill will show the correct aid credits.

- Get a handle on the cost of attendance for the academic year. By now, you should have selected your courses (setting the tuition and fee charge) and your room and board plan. Once your billable charges are known, organize a budget for books and personal expenses.

- Organize a plan for meeting your family financial responsibility. This entails knowing how much the student and parents will contribute to billable costs as well as who is going to cover books and personal expenses. If you are having trouble sorting this out, talk to an aid administrator. Do not wait until the start of classes to figure out how the bill will be paid.

- Do the paperwork for your student loan. (See the following section for student loan information.)

- Arrange for a summer job if one is expected by your college. Even if not required, you might want to work in the summer to earn extra money.

✔ If you have an academic-year job, find out more. Will you be assigned a position, or will you have to apply for a job when you get to campus? How many hours per week will you be working? Can you work more if you want to? What's the rate of pay? Do you receive a paycheck, or is the money credited to your account?

✔ If you have received a bill from the student accounts office, check to make sure your aid was properly credited.

# YOUR STUDENT LOAN

If you are a typical aid student, a good portion of your total package will be a loan. As gift aid, scholarships or grants aren't very complicated. You merely have to meet the requirements for renewal. A job is straightforward—you do the work and receive a paycheck. Loans, however, are a different matter. There is a lot you should know and a number of things that have to be done.

## The Loan Assignment

Your award letter will specify the amount and type of loan you have been given. Most likely, it will be a subsidized federal Stafford or Direct and/or a Perkins loan. All three types are good aid. If it is not clear whether the Stafford or Direct loan is subsidized, find out. (All Perkins loans are subsidized.)

If your loan is unsubsidized, it means that it is not need-based. If this is the case with your loan, you should check with an aid counselor to see what it would take for you to qualify for a subsidized loan. You will save considerable money if you don't have to pay the yearly interest.

## The Loan Application

The material that came with your award letter should have spelled out how to go about applying for your loan. A Stafford/Direct or Perkins application may have been included in the mailing, or there were instructions on how to get one.

Start the loan application process as soon as you can so the funds will be available to pay the college bill. If you wait, you may have to come up with extra money until the lender sends a check to the college.

## Loan Terms

Read the promissory note carefully so you understand what you are agreeing to. Pay particular attention to:

- The amount of the loan
- The interest rate
- Whether interest is due while you are in college
- When you begin to repay the loan
- The amount you owe each month
- The length of the repayment period
- If there are options other than a monthly repayment plan (for example, paying a percent of your income)
- The amount of up-front fees
- Whether some of your loan can be cancelled if you pursue certain occupations.

The advantage of loans is that they are readily available, and the application is easy to complete. The problem with student loans is that they are readily available, and the application is easy to complete.

Since you simply sign a promissory note and the money is paid to the college, it is not always obvious that you are getting a loan and not gift aid. Loans have to be repaid (there are severe penalties if you default), and many students are unaware of their monthly obligation as their loan total goes up each year.

> *Insider's Advice*: Although there will be exceptions, the best repayment method is to choose a monthly plan with a direct transfer from your bank to the holder of your loan note. A monthly plan allows you to build the expense into your budget. The automatic payment prevents defaults and usually lowers your interest rate because of incentives for on-time payment.
>
> Because of the serious consequences of defaulting on your loan (fines, withholding of wages, loss of credit rating), it is important that you know what you are getting into when you borrow. This means keeping track of your total obligation, translating that amount to a monthly payment, and estimating how your payments relate to future earnings.

## ALTERNATIVE AID SOURCES

These forms of additional financial assistance may be important if you are an aid student with a bill payment problem. If you are not on aid, these are the sources you can turn to if the money your family has available falls short of what is required.

You should always make an appeal to an aid administrator for more need-based funds before turning to alternative sources. Also, don't forget, whenever you start to think about how to find additional resources, you also want to look into ways to reduce your cost of attendance.

### Scholarships

Once you are enrolled in college and have chosen a major, it may pay to run an Internet scholarship search to see which awards appear. Also, visit your academic department to see if they award in-college scholarships or prizes.

If you have an interest in the military, visit the ROTC unit on campus. The commanding officer usually has a number of scholarships to award to enrolled students.

### Additional academic-year work

Some colleges have jobs left over after they place aid students in work-study. Check with the student employment office for on-campus positions as well as referrals to off-campus work.

### Unsubsidized loans, either federal or alternative

If you haven't already received the maximum Stafford or Direct loan, you are eligible to borrow an unsubsidized loan. The aid office can give you the application.

If you have already reached the yearly limit for a Stafford/Direct student loan, or you don't want a federal loan for some other reason, the financial aid office will have brochures that describe various alternative loan programs.

### Parental loans

When parents decide that they have to borrow to pay for college, the federal PLUS program is usually the first place they look. Currently, PLUS has an 7.72 percent interest rate, with a maximum of fourteen years to repay. Repayment begins sixty days after the money is received. There is no needs test, but there is a credit check. Parents can borrow up to the cost of education less financial aid.

Before you borrow a PLUS, it may be worthwhile to check out the terms of at least one alternative parent loan (once again, the aid office will have the information), a home equity line of credit, and other borrowing options, such as a life insurance policy or retirement plan.

# PAYMENT PLANS

These bill payment options don't give you any more aid, but they can help when you have a cash-flow problem and what you really need is more time to pay. If you find yourself in this position, go see a financial aid administrator or a staff member in student accounts and ask questions like:

- Does the college have a plan where I can stretch my payments out over a longer period of time?

- If not, can you recommend an external plan that will permit me to make smaller monthly payments?

Here are a few well-known companies that offer tuition payment plans:

- Academic Management Services: http://www.amsweb.com
- Key Education Resources: http://www.key.com/educate
- EduServ Technologies: http://www.eduserv.com

If you are unsuccessful in finding a solution to your cash-flow problem, ask if there is someone in the student accounts office with the authority to negotiate a plan that would meet your needs and be acceptable to the college.

## TUITION TAX CREDITS

Since Congress passed the 1997 Taxpayers' Relief Act, college financial aid is no longer limited to the usual categories of gift aid, loans, and work-study. There is now a fourth form of aid, called a tuition tax credit, that benefits families by reducing their tax bill.

---

*The difference between a tax deduction and a credit*

**A tax deduction** is an allowance against income *before* you figure how much you owe in taxes. If the deduction is $1,000 and you are in the 33 percent tax bracket, your actual benefit is $333. An example of a tax deduction is a contribution to a traditional IRA.

**A tax credit** is subtracted from your tax bill *at the end* of the process. If you are responsible for $5,000 in federal income tax and you are eligible for a $1,000 tax credit, you pay $4,000.

A tax credit is more advantageous then a tax deduction since it is a dollar-for-dollar benefit.

---

The two tuition tax credit programs that started with 1998 income are the **Hope Scholarship** (that's what it's called, but it isn't a scholarship) and the **Lifetime Learning Tax Credit**. In any year that you pay a tuition bill (including part-time course work), either for you or your dependents, the college is responsible to certify enrollment and advise you that you may be eligible to file an IRS form 8863 to claim a tax credit. If you want to find out more about the Hope and Lifetime Learning credits, the Web site at http://www.ed.gov/offices/ope/ppi/hope/ has details.

### Hope Scholarship

- You may apply for a credit for the first $1,000 of tuition expense and 50 percent of the next $1,000. (The maximum credit is $1,500.)
- It is good for the first two years of post-secondary education.
- Your Adjusted Gross Income can not be more than $50,000 if you file as a single person or $100,000 if you file a joint return.
- College attendence must be at least one-half time.
- If you do not pay taxes, you don't qualify.

### Lifetime Learning Credit

- An extension of the Hope Scholarship after the first two years of college.
- Includes graduate school and continuing education course work.
- You are able to claim as a tax credit 20 percent of tuition expense up to $5,000—a maximum of $1,000.
- The income limits are the same as the Hope.
- College attendance may be less than one-half time.

*Note:* Both the Hope Scholarship and the Lifetime Learning Credit have other restrictions, and some of the dollar amounts will increase based on inflation.

> *Insider's Advice*: If any family member attends college in a year in which you pay federal income taxes, consult a tax adviser about whether or not you are eligible for either the Hope Scholarship or the Lifetime Learning Credit.

## SUMMARY OF KEY POINTS

- Make sure you take all the steps necessary to finalize your aid award so the money can be credited to your bill.

- Have a plan for tying the family contribution to the cost of attendance. Figure out how much of the parent and student shares will go to pay the college bill and how books and personal expenses will be handled.

- Thoroughly review all aspects of your student loan before you sign the promissory note.

- Keep track of your monthly repayment obligation after graduation as you borrow more and more each year.

- If you feel you have to turn to alternative aid sources to help pay the bill, first check with an aid counselor for guidance and referral to the best programs.

- Don't forget about tuition tax credits. Although the money won't be available until later in the academic year, the maximum amount is equivalent to a $1,500 scholarship.

# CHAPTER 8

# Side Roads: Nontraditional Students

---

- Less than full-time
- Older undergraduates
- Graduate students
- Military veterans
- International students
- Distance learning
- Summary of key points

---

Perhaps it's time to redefine the term "traditional student." Today, less than one half of the college population is a dependent student between the ages of 18 and 22 attending full-time.

There are lots of part-time students, older undergraduates, and students in graduate school, and their numbers continue to grow. While much of the financial aid information presented up to this point holds true for all students, this chapter explains where there are differences you should know about.

## LESS THAN FULL-TIME

The basic rule for the awarding of most financial aid is that you must attend college at least one-half time. This includes eligibility for both federal loan programs—Direct and Stafford—as well as the Hope Scholarship tax credit explained in Chapter 7, page 114.

One-half time is defined as at least 6 semester hours per term, three-quarters time as 9 semester hours per term, and full-time as 12 semester hours per term. The amount of aid for which you qualify is reduced proportionately when you are less than a full-time student.

The only federal student aid for less than one-half-time attendance are

- Federal Pell Grants
- Lifetime Learning tax credit
- Supplemental grants (FSEOG)
- Perkins loans
- College Work-Study.

*Insider's Tip:* If you qualify for a Pell grant, you must receive the money. As a practical matter, you probably won't be awarded a Supplemental grant, Perkins loan, or Work-Study job, because colleges give these limited funds first to students attending full-time. It is unlikely any money will be left over for less than half-time students.

The large majority of state, college, and private scholarships and grants go to students who are attending college full-time. On occasion, there may be a scholarship for a part-time student, but almost always the scholarship requires at least half-time attendance.

*Insider's Tip:* Other than the possibility of getting a small Pell grant, you will find most financial aid doors closed if you are less than a one-half-time student. Although you will have a higher tuition bill, you may end up paying less if you attend college at least half-time and thereby qualify for aid.

# OLDER UNDERGRADUATES

If you are an adult attending college, there are differences in how you approach the aid process compared to an 18- to 22-year-old dependent student.

Similar to any college student who needs help paying educational costs, you want to start by searching for gift aid—scholarships and grants.

### Scholarships

If you haven't already done so, you should read Chapter 4, Reducing the Toll I: How to Find Scholarships.

You will find that relatively few scholarships have an age restriction, so technically you should be eligible for most of the same scholarships as a high school senior. Realistically, however, you will probably encounter some difficulties in your scholarship search.

The fundamental problem is that you are likely to be out of the secondary school loop and will have to make an extra effort to find out about scholarships and prepare an application.

Although not explicitly stated, most scholarship sponsors have in mind the 18-year-old twelfth grader when they set up their application procedures and selection criteria. Since you probably graduated from high school some years ago,

- it will be harder to get a transcript

- you may need to retake the SAT or ACT

- getting teacher recommendations will be difficult. (Perhaps you can substitute an employer's recommendation.)

*Insider's Tip:* Visit the college guidance counselor at your high school and ask for the same kind of assistance that would be available to a high school senior—access to scholarship information and help in preparing your credentials.

Although finding your way through the process will be somewhat more difficult than it will be for the twelfth grader who is inside the system, you have one advantage. Your application will stand out among those submitted by 18-year-olds with similar backgrounds. You will be able to write about richer personal and work experiences as well as articulate the importance of a college education to your career goals.

> ***Insider's Advice:*** Don't shy away from applying for scholarships because you are a nontraditional student. Take whatever steps are necessary to get inside the "scholarship loop." Once you start to apply for scholarships, your unique experiences and strong motivation to further your education will help make you a strong candidate for the award.

Peterson's publishes a reference book, *Peterson's Scholarships and Loans for Adult Students,* that presents a list of private scholarships open to older students.

### Education Benefits

A category that an adult student is more likely to qualify for than an 18- to 22-year-old is employer-provided tuition benefits. You should check with your human resource department about the availability of tuition assistance. Under current law, up to $5,250 that your employer pays toward undergraduate courses does not have to be counted as income.

### Grants

The application process for need-based aid is very similar to the one for a dependent student, with one major difference. When you fill out the FAFSA (and PROFILE, if required), your Expected Family Contribution (EFC) will be calculated on your (and your spouse's) financial information.

> **Insider's Advice:** As an older undergraduate or graduate student aid applicant, it is likely that your parents' information will be excluded from the need calculation. You will find, however, that certain colleges and graduate schools have their own rules defining independent student status. It might be important to know about this policy before you apply. If, for example, your parents no longer plan to pay any money toward your education, you may want to think twice about applying to a college or graduate school that expects them to contribute even though you are federally independent.

If you are **federally independent**, your parental information is not required. To receive this status, you must meet at least one of the following standards:

- be 24 years old by December 31 of the calendar year that begins the academic year in which you plan to enroll. *For example, for the 2000–2001 academic year, you must have your twenty-fourth birthday by December 31, 2000*

- be an orphan or ward of the court

- be a veteran of the U.S. Armed Forces

- be married or have dependents other than a spouse

- be a graduate student

- be judged independent by a financial aid administrator based on special circumstances.

These are the independent student rules for the awarding of federal student aid. As is the case in other areas of financial assistance, most state and college aid programs use the same standards to judge if you are self-supporting.

There are, however, exceptions. Many of the colleges that require PROFILE (because they award large amounts of their own money) do not accept the federal definition of independence and will ask for more information before they decide whether or not to waive the requirement that your parents submit financial data. The same holds true for some graduate schools. *For example, it is common practice for medical schools to ask for parental financial information from all their aid applicants.*

# GRADUATE STUDENTS

*Note:* Sometimes you will see a distinction made between graduate and professional students based on the type of graduate school. Schools of law, business, medicine, and architecture are called "professional," while other courses of study are termed "graduate." For the sake of simplicity, I have used the term graduate student for anyone engaged in postsecondary education.

There are differences in terminology between undergraduate and graduate aid. At the graduate level,

- Gift aid that covers tuition is called a fellowship
- Gift aid to pay for living expenses is a stipend (although some large fellowships may include a stipend)
- A job is called an assistantship when it involves teaching or research
- A loan is still a loan.

There is relatively little need-based gift aid for graduate students. Fellowships are usually given based on merit. Need comes into play if the combination of fellowship, stipend, and assistantship does not cover your cost of attendance. The cost of attendance calculation is more complicated for graduate students, since there may be expenses to support a spouse and children.

If you need additional assistance beyond what you receive from the graduate school, you complete a FAFSA to see if you qualify for a Stafford, Direct, or Perkins loan.

A graduate student is automatically classified as federally independent. When you complete the FAFSA (graduate students use the same form as undergraduates), you will not have to show your parents' financial information. If you have a spouse, his or her income and assets are included.

With the possible exception of graduate study in the sciences and engineering, where fellowships, stipends, and assistantships are more generous, expect to have to borrow to pay for graduate school. Loans are much more common (and the yearly amounts larger) for graduate school than for undergraduate study.

If you demonstrate need, the subsidized Stafford or Direct loan is your best bet. The next place to go is either the unsubsidized Stafford or Direct loan (provided you still have federal eligibility) or an alternative loan. Alternative loans are a major aid source for graduate study. In fact, these alternative loans are so prevalent that programs have been designed to meet the needs of students studying in specific areas. There are medical loans, law loans, M.B.A. loans, graduate access loans, engineering loans, and so on.

In general, if you run up a big loan tab for professional school (medicine, business, and law), your future earning potential is high enough for you to be able to repay your loan and end up ahead in the long run. The real difficulty occurs when you borrow a lot and your income is modest. This can occur in graduate school programs like social work. These are the situations where loan repayments become unmanageable and serious financial problems follow, including the possibility of default.

Before you decide to attend graduate school, you should work out a careful financial plan, especially how much you will have to repay on your loans.

Non-university fellowships or grants are available and eagerly sought. Publications providing directories to these programs, such as the *Annual Register of Grant Support* and the *Grants Register* can be found in many libraries. Among major fellowship sponsors are

- **National Research Council Fellowship Office:** http://www4. nas.edu/osep/fo.nsf

- **Woodrow Wilson Foundation:** http://www.woodrow.org

- **National Science Foundation:** http://www.nsf.gov
- **Social Science/Humanities Research Council:** http://www.sshrc.org
- **Social Science Research Council:** http://www.ssrc.org
- **Alfred P. Sloan Foundation:** http://www.sloan.org
- **Harry S. Truman Scholarships:** http://www.truman.gov
- **National Defense Science and Engineering Fellowships:** http://www.battelle.org/ndseg
- **National Physical Science Consortium:** http://www.npsc.org
- **Jacob J. Javits Fellowships:** http://www.ed.gov/offices/OPE/HEP/iegps/javits.html
- **Mellon Foundation:** http://www.woodrow.org/mellon
- **Fulbright Fellowships:** http://www.fulbright.org/scholarship
- **GAANN—Guaranteed Access in Areas of National Need Traineeships:** http://www.ed.gov/offices/OPE/HEP/iegps
- **National Consortium for Graduate Education for Minorities (GEM):** http://www.nd.edu/~gem
- **EPA/STAR Fellowships:** http://www.es.epa.goc/ncerqa/tfa
- **Foreign Affairs Fellowship Program (FAFP):** http://www.woodrow.org/public-policy/gfaf
- **Ford Foundation Predoctoral Fellowship:** http://www2.nas.edu/fo
- **Foreign Language Area Studies (FLAS) Fellowships:** http://www.ed.gov/offices/OPE/HEP/iegps

# MILITARY VETERANS

Your status as a former member of the U.S. Armed Forces opens the door to more aid possibilities than any other single category. The GI Bill is a very large aid program, and there are many other scholarships earmarked for veterans.

*Note:* If you are interested in financial aid you receive before you serve in the military, see Chapter 4, pages 64–65, about the service academies and the Reserve Officer Training Corps (ROTC) scholarship program.

## Montgomery GI Bill

This is the current name for the education benefits that a member of the military earns as a result of serving on active duty in the U.S. Armed Forces.

Prior to 1976, it was called the GI Bill; from 1976 to 1985, the Veteran's Education Assistance Program (VEAP); and since 1985, the Montgomery GI Bill.

The basic rules are

- the benefit is good for almost any type of further education
- to receive the maximum benefit, you must serve at least three years of active duty or two years plus four years in the Selected Reserve or National Guard
- you must have a high school diploma
- you must use the benefits within ten years
- you will have $100 per month for the first twelve months deducted from your paycheck
- you must receive an honorable discharge.

The education payments for full service are $416 per month for up to thirty-six months. Those who serve less will receive $338 per month. In addition to these amounts, individual services may provide extra money to encourage enlistment in areas of critical need.

The Veterans Administration Web site has full details about GI Bill benefits at http://www.va.gov/education/C30.htm.

## Other Scholarships for Veterans

I suggest a four-step approach to look for these scholarships.

1. Enter your personal information in one of the scholarship search programs that are available for free on the Internet and see which scholarships come up.

2. Pick up a copy of *Need a Lift?*, 43rd edition, 1993, which is available from the American Legion. This is the best printed publication for sources of financial aid for veterans, and the price is right. Send $3.00 to the American Legion, National Emblem Sales, P.O. Box 1050, Indianapolis, Indiana 46206.

3. Check with your state department of veteran affairs or the office of student assistance to see whether there are state aid programs specifically designed for military veterans. A list of these offices is located in Appendix B.

4. Once you've made your college list, read the financial aid section of the admission material to see if there are scholarships for veterans. Even if there is no mention, it may still be worthwhile to call the financial aid office to double check.

--- ◇ ---

## INTERNATIONAL STUDENTS

If you are a student from another country, it will be difficult to get aid from U.S. sources. It is estimated that 80 percent of international undergraduates and one half of all international graduate students pay for college costs from resources within their own country, either family or government.

What little aid there is from within the U.S. is likely to come from college funds. While most U.S. colleges only have a small amount—perhaps an occasional academic or athletic scholarship—some colleges seek to attract international students through strong aid programs. A list of these colleges can be found at http://www.finaid.org by clicking on "eduPASS," then "Financing College," then "Schools with Financial Aid for International Undergraduate Students."

The main source of information about studying in the U.S. is the Institute for International Education (IIE). Their financial aid publication is "Funding for U.S. Study—A Guide for International Students and Professionals" (Web site: http://www.iie.org). Another helpful site is the eduPASS section of http://www.finaid.org.

*Note:* Although Canadian students are not eligible for US government money and most private scholarships, a number of colleges do not distinguish between Canadian and U.S. citizens when they award their own aid funds. Check with the college financial aid office for their policy.

———————————— ◇ ————————————

## DISTANCE LEARNING

This term applies to students who take courses from a location that is some distance from the college campus. Until recently, the primary method was to take correspondence courses by mail. Today, distance learning usually refers to courses taken over the Internet.

The basic financial aid rules for distance learners are the same as for residential students—be enrolled in a degree program at an accredited college at least one-half time. But there is one further restriction that applies to distance learners. To receive federal aid, the college must meet the 50 percent standard. This means that the college can offer no more than one half of its courses by telecommunications or correspondence. In other words, "virtual" institutions (those that are entirely Internet-based) do not qualify for federal aid, except for a handful of colleges that are participating in the Distance Education Demonstration Project.

> ***Insider's Advice:*** Before you sign up for distance learning courses, make sure your program qualifies for federal student aid.

# SUMMARY OF KEY POINTS

- If you need aid as a part-time student, arrange your schedule so you are at least half-time.

- You cannot just declare yourself independent so that your parents don't have to pay for college. You must meet the federal guidelines.

- If you enlist in the military, a down payment of $1,200 will give you many times that in education benefits under the GI Bill.

# CHAPTER 9

# If You Still Have Questions

- Free advice
- Fee-based advice

Hopefully, you've received a lot of helpful advice in the preceding eight chapters. If there is one thing I've learned in my experience in the financial aid profession, it's that there are as many students and parents with special circumstances as there are standard cases.

While the *Insider's Guide* has undoubtedly answered many of your questions, it may have raised some as well. If this applies to you, I'd like to mention where you can go to receive further assistance.

## FREE ADVICE

### Your High School Guidance Office

I mention this first because much of the financial aid process starts in the high school. This is the primary location for scholarship postings and information on how to apply for aid. After providing this basic function as part of their college guidance role, the ability to help further with financial aid matters varies widely from one high school to another.

Some high schools have a counselor who is the financial aid person and can guide you through the process, much the same way he or she can help you organize your admission application.

Other high schools, after they post the FAFSA procedures, do very little else. It may be because they don't have the staff to do any more than provide the most basic information or because they are reluctant to get involved in any aspect of a family's financial situation.

> ***Insider's Advice:*** As you start the financial aid process, whether it is searching for scholarships or finding out more about need aid, stop by your high school guidance office and see what help they can give you. In addition, you should visit your local library and ask about the college financial aid section. If your high school guidance office only provides basic information, the town library may be a better source of aid material.

## The Federal Government

The U.S. Department of Education operates the majority of the federal student aid programs. They have a number of customer service telephone numbers, depending on the subject of your question. The following are U.S. Department of Education Help Lines:

- **FAFSA processing.** Receive a FAFSA, get help with completion of the form, check on processing status, or change college choices (800-433-3243, toll-free).

- **FAFSA electronic applications.** Get assistance with FAFSA on the Web, renewal FAFSA on the Web, and FAFSA Express (800-801-0576, toll-free).

- **Direct loans.** Provide new information, obtain account information, or discuss repayment problems (800-848-0979, toll-free).

- **Combine various loans into one.** Get information on loan consolidation (800-557-7394, toll-free).

- **Defaulted student loans.** If you have defaulted on a loan held by the federal government, find out what is owed and discuss a repayment plan (800-621-3115, toll-free).

## Your State Aid Programs

If you have a question about a scholarship, grant, or loan sponsored by your state, you can contact the department of higher education (sometimes called the office of student assistance or state grant or loan agency) by phone or through the Internet. See the list of State Higher Education Agencies in Appendix A.

## A Financial Aid Professional

You may have a question that is too complicated (or too personal) to ask a high school guidance counselor or one that doesn't refer to a specific federal or state aid program. These other types of questions can best be answered by a financial aid administrator.

If your question refers to aid policies or procedures at a particular college, get in touch with the campus financial aid office. If your question is of a routine nature, for example about a deadline or form requirement, a phone call (or e-mail) is recommended.

If your question is more involved, for example you are requesting special consideration or you want to support your application with additional information, a personal visit is the preferred means of contact.

If your question is more general and it doesn't involve an application to a college on your list, you might try a financial aid administrator at a local college or use Internet e-mail to ask an expert.

- **http://www.finaid.com**  This site has signed up more than 100 aid professionals to volunteer their time to respond to questions. Click on "Ask the Aid Advisor," and enter your question in the space provided. An answer is promised within two weeks.

- **http://www.salliemae.com**  Sallie Mae, the large education service company, primarily deals with student and parent loans, but their financial aid experts have been trained to answer a variety of questions. Click on "Students/Parents," click on "Ask College Answer," and click on college.answer@slma.com, and you will see an e-mail form on which to enter your question. You can also ask your question over the phone at 800-239-4269 (toll-free), Monday through Friday, 8 a.m. to 11 p.m. EST.

- **http://www.collegequest.com**   This is the site developed by Peterson's to assist students in the college-going process. It covers both admission and financial aid subject matter and has three experts available to field questions. Register, click on "Advice Center," and click on "Expert Forum." The drawback of this site compared to finaid.org and salliemae.com is that not every question is answered.

# FEE-BASED ADVICE

Nearly all of you should be able to understand and deal with the financial aid system by reading the material contained in the *Insider's Guide* and going to the appropriate Internet site when you need more information.

Some of you will have specific questions about a college's aid policies or want to check on the status of your FAFSA or other aid application. The staff in the financial aid office or the customer service representatives at the federal or state processing center should be able to give you the answers you need.

All of the sources of information described in the previous section are free, and, in general, I don't recommend that you pay money to someone to guide you through the financial aid process. However, if you have tried the sources I mentioned and still feel the need for further advice, you should be cautious about whom you pay for  help.

Here are my comments about fee-based advice in different areas.

## College Savings

Making the right decision about how to set up a college savings plan is complicated since you have to weigh investment strategies, understand complex tax rules, be aware of varying treatments under the need formula, and so forth. This is an area in which it may be worthwhile to spend some money to get advice, since the difference in the bottom-line payoff between a good savings plan and a poorly structured one can be thousands of dollars.

> **Insider's Advice:** Check with both an account representative at a major financial institution and a certified financial planner. See how much they know about the intricacies of college savings plans (including how savings are viewed in the need formula) and how much they charge for their service.

## Scholarship Search and Other Promises of Getting You More Money

This is where I would be most cautious about paying a fee for assistance. Since nearly all well-organized scholarship databases contain essentially the same awards, and many are available on the Internet for free (see Chapter 3, pages 44–47), there is no longer any reason to pay money for a scholarship search.

Because the fee-based scholarship search business has lost its value, these companies have shifted their sales pitch to "guarantee full funding" or help you "beat the financial aid system."

Since only the college financial aid office or a legitimate scholarship sponsor can set the size of your aid, the "guarantee" is usually no more than telling you about the federal PLUS loan, where your parents can borrow up to the full cost of education.

"Beating the financial aid system" usually translates into telling you how to juggle some of the figures on the FAFSA to increase your aid eligibility. While there are some aspects of completing the FAFSA that you should know about (see Chapter 4, pages 83–86), there are federal penalties if you give information that is false or misleading.

Other indicators that the scholarship search company is disreputable are high cost (one firm I recently encountered was charging $900), arm-twisting sales techniques, and precharging your credit card.

While there may be a few legitimate companies in the business of getting you more financial aid through one technique or another, I would not recommend spending any money (or signing a contract) until you have a college financial aid administrator review their material and approve their service. As it turns out, one of the most common areas of complaint for the Federal Trade Commission is the "scholarship scam" business. If you want to learn more, http//www.finaid.org has a good summary. Click on "Scholarships" and then "common scholarship scams."

## Certified Financial Planners

I mentioned above that it might be worthwhile to look into the services that a certified financial planner offers about financing a college education. Some certified planners have also studied the financial aid process and may be able to offer assistance there as well. It is likely that your state or county has an association of certified financial planners. By calling their phone number, you will be able to get a referral or two.

> *Insider's Advice:* In general, you should look for a "fee-only financial planner." Most of these are also Certified Financial Planners, or CFPs. ("Fee-only" means the planner receives income from the services provided to you, not from commissions on other products, like life insurance.) For a list of fee-only financial advisers in your area, call or write to the National Association of Personal Financial Advisers (NAPFA), 355 West Dundee Road, Suite 200, Buffalo Grove, Illinois 60089 (telephone: 800-333-6659, toll free).

Before you sign a contract with a financial planner, be sure to get references from other customers. I also recommend that you ask a local financial aid administrator what he or she thinks of the price for what is promised. Perhaps the aid administrator will offer to do the same thing for nothing.

# Appendix A

## STATE HIGHER EDUCATION OFFICES

State student financial aid programs include loans, scholarships, grants, survivors' benefits, and college savings programs. Each state's programs are organized differently.

Here is a list of state higher education offices and their Web sites. If these offices do not administer all of the state programs directly, they can serve as a clearinghouse for information about which state agency runs which program.

**Alabama Commission on Higher Education**
http://www.ache.state.al.us/finaidb

**Alaska Commission on Postsecondary Education**
http://www.state.ak.us/acpe/student.html

**Arizona Commission for Postsecondary Education**
http://www.acpe.asu.edu/programs/

**Arkansas Department of Higher Education**
http://www.arscholarships.com

**California Student Aid Commission**
http://www.csac.ca.gov

**Colorado Commission on Higher Education**
http://www.state.co.us/cche_dir/hecche.html

**Connecticut Department of Higher Education**
http://ctdhe.commnet.edu/dheweb

**Delaware Higher Education Commission**
http://www.doe.state.de.us/high-ed/scholar.htm

**Department of Human Services, Office of Postsecondary Education, Research and Assistance**
http://www.cl.washington.dc.us

**Florida Department of Education, Office of Student Financial Assistance**
http://www.firn.edu/doe/bin00065/home0065.htm

**Georgia Student Finance Commission, State Loans and Grants Division**
http://www.gsfc.org

**University of Guam**
http://uog2.uog.edu/trio/index.html

**Hawaii State Postsecondary Education Commission**
http://dbserver.its.hawaii.edu/cash/

**Idaho Board of Education**
http://www.sde.state.id.us/osbe/board.htm

**Illinois Student Assistance Commission**
http://www.isac-online.org

**State Student Assistance Commission of Indiana**
http://www.state.in.us/ssaci/

**Iowa College Student Aid Commission**
http://www.state.ia.us/collegeaid/

**Kansas Board of Regents**
http://www.ukans.edu/~kbor

**Kentucky Higher Education Assistance Authority**
http://www.khea.state.ky.us

**Louisiana Office of Student Financial Assistance**
http://www.osfa.state.la.us

**Finance Authority of Maine, Education Assistance Division**
http://www.famemaine.com.

**Maryland Higher Education Commission**
http://www.ubalt.edu/www/mhec

**Massachusetts Office of Student Financial Assistance**
http://www.osfa.mass.edu/

**Michigan Higher Education Assistance Authority, Office of Scholarships and Grants**
http://www.treas.state.mi.us/college/mheaa.htm

**Minnesota Higher Education Services Office**
http://www.heso.state.mn.us

**Mississippi Office of State Student Financial Aid**
http://www.mhc.state.ms.us/financial_aid.html

**Missouri Coordinating Board for Higher Education**
http://www.mocbhe.gov/mostars/finmenu.htm

**Montana University System**
http://www.montana.edu/wwwoche/docs/assistance.html

**Coordinating Commission for Postsecondary Education (Nebraska)**
http://www.nol.org/nepostsecondaryed

**University and Community College System of Nevada**
http://www.nevada.edu/

**New Hampshire Postsecondary Education Commission**
http://www.state.nh.us/postsecondary

**New Jersey Higher Education Student Assistance Authority**
http://www.state.nj.us/treasury/osa/

**Commission on Higher Education (New Mexico)**
http://www.nmche.org/

**New York State Higher Education Services Corporation**
http://www.hesc.com

**North Carolina State Education Assistance Authority**
http://www.ncseaa.edu

**North Dakota University System, North Dakota Student Financial Assistance Program**
http://www.ndus.nodak.edu/student_info/financial_aid.html

**Ohio Board of Regents**
http://www.regents.state.oh.us/sgs/

**Oklahoma State Regents for Higher Education, Oklahoma Tuition Aid Grant Program**
http://www.okhighered.org

**Oregon State Scholarship Commission**
http://www.ossc.state.or.us/index.html

**Pennsylvania Higher Education Assistance Agency**
http://www.pheaa.org

**Council on Higher Education (Puerto Rico)**
http://www.prstar.net

**Rhode Island Higher Education Assistance Authority**
http://www.riheaa.org/

**South Carolina Higher Education Tuition Grants Commission**
http://www.state.sc.us/tuitiongrants/

**South Dakota Board of Regents**
http://www.ris.sdbor.edu

**Tennessee Higher Education Commission**
http://www.state.tn.us/tsac

**Texas Higher Education Coordinating Board**
http://www.thecb.state.tx.us/otherrecs/finaidrec.htm

**Utah State Board of Regents, Utah System of Higher Education**
http://www.uheaa.org

**Vermont Student Assistance Corporation**
http://www.vsac.org

**State Council of Higher Education for Virginia**
http://www.schev.edu/wufinaid/sumprog.html

**Virgin Islands Board of Education**
http://www.usvi.org/education/index.html

**Washington State Higher Education Coordinating Board**
http://www.hecb.wa.gov/paying/index.html

**State College and University Systems of West Virginia, Central Office**
http://www.scusco.wvnet.edu/

**Higher Educational Aids Board (Wisconsin)**
http://www.heab.state.wi.us

**State of Wyoming/University of Wyoming Office of Student Financial Aid**
http://siswww.uwyo.edu/sfa/schlbook/chap1.html

# Appendix B

## VETERANS AFFAIRS OFFICES

Education benefits for military service are among the most commonly encountered forms of aid for higher education study. The Montgomery GI Bill can provide the largest potential benefit to veterans. The Veterans Administration Web site has details (http://www.va.gov/education/C30.htm).

The American Legion and American Legion auxiliaries have been active in establishing scholarships for veterans and their children and spouses. There are some national awards, but most are offered by state American Legion departments. Qualifications vary from program to program and, in addition to state residence, may include membership in the American Legion, service in a war, or service-related disability or death. A list of American Legion Department Web sites can be found at http://www.legion.org/dept.htm. The Legion also publishes *Need a Lift?*, which is available for $3 from the American Legion, National Emblem Sales, P.O. Box 1050, Indianapolis, Indiana 46206. This publication provides a good summary of available educational benefits for veterans and their immediate families.

Many states have programs that provide full or partial tuition benefits to veterans and/or their immediate family members. Qualifications and awards vary. Below is a list of state offices of veterans' affairs and their Web sites. While not all of these offices provide assistance directly, they usually can provide information about educational benefits that are available to resident veterans and their families.

**Alabama State Department of Veterans' Affairs**
http://www.state.al.us/dva

**Alaska Division of Military and Veterans Affairs**
http://www.ngchak.org/dmva/

**Arizona State Veterans Commission**
http://www.azvets.com/avsc.html

**Arkansas Department of Veterans' Affairs**
http://www.state.ar.us/directory/detail2.cgi?ID=106

**California Department of Veterans Affairs**
http://www.ns.net/cadva/

**Colorado Division of Veterans Affairs, Department of Human Services**
http://www.cdhs.state.co.us/ods/dva

**Connecticut Department of Veterans' Affairs**
http://www.state.ct.us/ctva

**Delaware Commission of Veterans Affairs**
http://www.state.de.us/veteran/index.htm

**District of Columbia, U.S. Veterans Administration**
http://www.va.gov

**Florida Department of Veterans' Affairs**
http://fcn.state.fl.us/fdva/

**Georgia Department of Veterans Service**
http://www2.state.ga.us/Departments/Veterans/

**Guam Veterans Affairs Office, Office of the Governor**
no Web site

**Hawaii Department of Defense, Office of Veterans Services**
http://web-server.dod.state.hi.us/OVS/

**Idaho State Veterans Services**
http://www.state.id.us/dhw/hwgd_www/vetserv/index.html

**IH2inois Department of Veterans Affairs**
http://www.state.il.us/dva

**Indiana Department of Veterans Affairs**
http://www.ai.org/veteran/index.html

**Iowa Commission of Veterans Affairs**
http://www.sos.state.ia.us/register/r4/r4vetaff.htm

**Kansas Commission on Veterans Affairs**
no Web site

**Kentucky Department of Veterans Affairs**
http://www.state.ky.us/agencies/military/

**Louisiana Department of Veterans Affairs**
http://www.state.la.us

**Bureau of Maine Veterans' Services**
http://www.state.me.us/va/defense/hmpgmvs.htm

**Maryland Veterans Commission**
http://www.gov.state.md.us./mvc/

**Massachusetts Department of Veteran Services**
no Web site

**Michigan Department of Military and Veterans Affairs**
http://www.state.mi.us/dmva/

**Minnesota Department of Veterans Affairs**
http://www.mdva.state.mn.us/

**Mississippi State Veterans Affairs Board**
http://www.vab.state.ms.us/

**Missouri Veterans Commission**
http://www.dps.state.mo.us/dps/mvc/

**Montana Department of Military Affairs, Veterans' Affairs Division**
http://www.state.mt.us/dma

**Nebraska Department of Veterans Affairs**
http://www.hhs.state.ne.us/ags/vets.htm

**Nevada Commission for Veterans Affairs**
http://www.state.nv.us/veterans/

**New Hampshire State Veterans Council**
http://www.state.nh.us/nhveterans/

**New Jersey Department of Military and Veterans Affairs**
http://www.state.ny.us/veterans/

**New Mexico Veterans[0092] Service Commission**
http://www.state.nm.us/veterans/

**New York Division of Veterans Affairs**
http://www.veterans.state.ny.us/

**North Carolina Division of Veterans Affairs**
http://www.doa.state.nc.us/vets/vahome.htm

**North Dakota Department of Veterans' Affairs**
http://www.state.nd.us/jsnd/vetdept.htm

**Ohio Governor's Office of Veterans Affairs**
http://www.state.oh.us/gova/

**Oklahoma Department of Veterans Affairs**
http://www.odva.state.ok.us/

**Oregon Department of Veterans Affairs**
http://www.odva.state.or.us/

**Pennsylvania Department Of Military and Veterans Affairs**
http://www.state.pa.us/PA_Exec/Military_Affairs/bio.htm

**Puerto Rico Public Advocate for Veterans Affairs**
no Web site

**Rhode Island Veterans Affairs Division**
http://www.dhs.state.ri.us

**South Carolina Office of Veterans' Affairs**
http://www.state.sc.us/oepp/vetaff.htm

**South Dakota Department of Military and Veterans Affairs**
http://www.state.sd.us/state/executive/military/military.html

**Tennessee Department of Veterans Affairs**
http://www.state.tn.us/veteran/

**Texas Veterans Commission**
http://www.main.org/tvc/

**Utah Division of Veterans Affairs**
http://www.ce.ex.state.ut.us/veterans/welcome.htm

**Vermont Veterans' Program**
http://www.dad.state.vt.us/dvr/Veterans/vp.htm

**Virginia Department of Veterans Affairs**
http://www.va.gov/education

**Virgin Islands Division of Veterans' Affairs**
http://www.gov.vi/viva/

**Washington Department of Veterans' Affairs**
http://www.wa.gov/dva/

**West Virginia Division of Veterans' Affairs**
no Web site

**Wisconsin Department of Veterans Affairs**
http://badger.state.wi.us/agencies/dva/

**Wyoming Veterans Affairs Council**
http://www.state.wy.us/governor/boards/veterans/veterans.html

# NOTES

# NOTES

# NOTES

# NOTES

# NOTES

# NOTES

# NOTES

# NOTES

# Peterson's is on your side with everything you need to get ready for college!

## Get on line at petersons.com for a jump start on your college search.

- Search our college database
- Get financial aid tips
- Browse our bookstore

## And when you're ready to apply, you're ready for CollegeQuest.com℠!

CollegeQuest.com is our **free** online college application service that lets you apply to *more colleges than anyone else on the Internet!*

## Why CollegeQuest.com?

- Fill out one application for 1,200 colleges!
- Talk with admissions deans!
- It's FREE!

www.petersons.com
Keyword on AOL: Petersons
800-338-3282

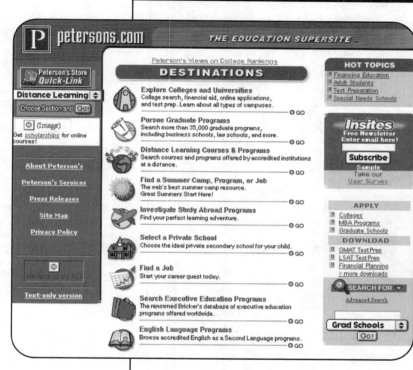

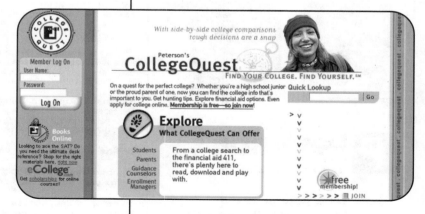